Interp
the
Parables

Interpreting the Parables

Parables

A Hermeneutical Guide to Their Meaning

John W. Sider

ZondervanPublishingHouse
Grand Rapids, Michigan

A Division of HarperCollinsPublishers

Interpreting the Parables
Copyright © 1995 by John W. Sider

Requests for information should be addressed to:
Zondervan Publishing House
Grand Rapids, Michigan 49530

Library of Congress Cataloging-in-Publication Data

Sider, John W.
    Interpreting the parables : a hermeneutical guide to their meaning
/ John W. Sider.
      p. cm.
    Includes bibliographical references and index.
    ISBN: 0-310-49451-6
    1. Jesus Christ—Parables. 2. Parables. 3. Analogy. I. Title.
BT375.2.S54 1995
226.8'06—dc20
                                        95-11005
                                        CIP

Edited by Patti Picardi
Interior design by Sherri L. Hoffman

Printed in the United States of America

95 96 97 98 99 00 / ❖ DH / 10 9 8 7 6 5 4 3 2 1

Dedicated to
Philip, Rebecca, and Sonya

CONTENTS

PART 2

Internal Features of the Parables

PREFACE

Like most cross-disciplinary ventures, this book needs some explanation. When Moisés Silva proposed a hermeneutical guide to the parables for college and seminary students, we knew it would not be a conventional textbook in either content or method. Encountering parable criticism as an English teacher, I had found a theory of allegory quite at odds with my experience of literary works from many times and places. Whereas we expect basic textbooks to stick to well-known territory, and to survey the subject from familiar perspectives by familiar methods, this book challenges conventional wisdom about the parables and employs methods more familiar in English literature classes than in courses on biblical hermeneutics.

The experience of one discipline can be useful in another, but scholars in biblical and nonbiblical literature have significantly different habits of thinking and writing. In my attempt to bridge the gap, I am deeply grateful for the help of Moisés Silva and of Zondervan editors James Ruark and Patti Picardi.

Students of Westmont College in a decade of Literary Analysis classes have helped me develop concepts and methods of this book—my thanks to them all, and to Joel and Michelle Pelsue, my tutorial students in an experiment with part 1. My thanks are due also to George V. Blankenbaker, academic dean of Westmont College, for sabbatical time; to Robert Gundry for advice and encouragement; to Ned Divelbiss and Diane Ziliotto for many favors in bibliographic reference; and to Zachary Taylor Ralston for introducing me to Cardinal Cajetan and the analogy of proportionality. My greatest debt is to my wife, Anna.

ACKNOWLEDGMENTS

The author gratefully acknowledges use of material from the following sources:

"Proportional Analogy in the Gospel Parables," by John W. Sider, *New Testament Studies* 31 (1985): 1–23, © 1985, Cambridge University Press. Reprinted with the permission of Cambridge University Press.

B.C. by Johnny Hart, copyright © Field Enterprises, Inc., 1977. Reprinted by permission of Johnny Hart and Creators Syndicate, Inc.

Poet and Peasant by Kenneth Ewing Bailey, copyright © 1976 by William B. Eerdmans Publishing Company. Reprinted by permission.

Through Peasant Eyes by Kenneth Ewing Bailey, copyright © 1980 by William B. Eerdmans Publishing Company, reprinted by permission.

Matthew: A Commentary on His Literary and Theological Art by Robert H. Gundry, copyright © 1982 by William B. Eerdmans Publishing Company, reprinted by permission.

The Gospel in Parable by John R. Donahue, copyright © 1988 by Fortress Press. Reprinted by permission of Augsburg Fortress.

The Parables by Dan O. Via, copyright © 1967 by Fortress Press. Used by permission of Augsburg Fortress.

Hear Then the Parable by Bernard Brandon Scott, copyright © 1989 Augsburg Fortress. Reprinted by permission.

The Parables in the Gospels: History and Allegory by John Drury, copyright © 1985 by John Drury. Printed by permission of the Crossroad Publishing Co., New York.

INTRODUCTION

A generation ago one interpreter of the parables of Jesus found humorous irony in another interpreter's tendency, in spite of himself, to read a parable allegorically (Black, 283, on the Tenants):

> While thus showing allegory firmly to the door, one cannot but wonder if Dr. Dodd has not surreptitiously smuggled it in again by the window. . . . [He] manages to get the benefit of allegory while denying that it is allegory—to run with the allegorical hare, as it were, and still hunt with the Jülicher hounds.

Dodd's "smuggling" was certainly inadvertent, for he vigorously denied the presence of allegory in Jesus' parables. Though the great majority of interpreters agreed with him, a few scholars such as Baird, Brown, and Hunter (115–17) thought otherwise. Nowadays more and more interpreters (e.g., Blomberg, 29–69) are rightly repudiating as untenable Jülicher's century-old distinction between *parable* as a realistic story with one point and *allegory* as an unrealistic story with many points. One may find ample corroboration of this judgment in the record of a broad range of ancient and modern literature, which bears witness to the customary merging of parable and allegory as the two have traditionally been defined and distinguished in parable criticism.

Why did interpreters such as Dodd and Jeremias unintentionally allegorize the parables, in spite of their commitment to the one-point theory? They were responding to the real meaning of the parables, and their tacit instincts and reflexes as interpreters were more reliable than their avowed theory—though the theory often hampered their observations of a parable's way of meaning. Meanwhile the general practice of critics working with nonbiblical literature acknowledged no such sharp distinction between parable and allegory.

One reason for this anomaly is that the standard methods of biblical interpretation—including Jülicher's ideas about parable and allegory—had already been established by the time the academic study of modern literatures such as English became commonplace little more than a century ago. For a long time parable studies proceeded largely in isolation from scholarship in nonbiblical literature. A second reason is that many biblical scholars have not read widely enough in nonbiblical literature to see for themselves how artificial is the distinction of parable and allegory. Further, recent biblical scholarship has been hindered by its greater attention to literary *theory* than to the *practice* of literary critics. Critical practice, as we will see, would be a more useful precedent for interpreting the Bible than critical theory. Finally, biblical scholars have received very little help, in either theory or practice, from scholars of literature in general (Sider 1981, 15). Few people outside the field of biblical scholarship have published any response to what biblical scholars say about the parables.

CRITICAL THEORY VERSUS CRITICAL PRACTICE

Therefore biblical scholars might wish to know what is the consensus of general literary criticism about the parables, but unfortunately no consensus exists. The practical criticism in our literary journals illustrates this lack of consensus about how literature in general should be read, or what its chief value is. Most practical critics know and profit from the succession of literary theories that this century has produced, but without radically altering their praxis in accord with each new theory. If one looks at our journals rather than listening to our common talk about the prestige of theory, it is obvious that praxis has not been dominated by the latest theory. Thus, biblical scholars cannot ascertain our critical praxis by reading our theory, while those least familiar with our praxis are the most likely to assume that they can. Since there is no consensus, this book cannot be *the* literary perspective on the parables, but simply *a* literary perspective, one that depends on the evidence of the parable texts for its credibility.

How do scholars in English and other modern languages develop their principles of praxis for literature in general? Most are not concerned primarily with aesthetics—that is, with considerations of beautiful form and style—much as they defend the validity of that approach. They invoke aesthetics mainly as a means: for the history of ideas, for psychology, sociology, religion—with politics recently having come to the fore. More important, like the best biblical scholars, they do not rely solely on one literary theory—or even an eclectic combination—as their tool for all texts. Rather than deductively applying a preconceived theory to every text, they devise, *by inductive observation,* tools especially suited to each individual text. Such sensitive and individual regard for what is in the literary texts characterizes much of practical criticism's interpretive studies.

Eclectic improvisation is the common-sense principle that guides automotive toolmakers in devising new tools for new cars, and that guides the physicist in inventing new math to deal with new questions. In the praxis of general literary criticism this eclectic improvisation creates a cutting edge of a different sort from the cutting edge of the theorists, and one that may be more immediately beneficial to interpretation. In both disciplines, literary and biblical, the talk about methods is dominated, understandably, by natural-born theorists like Frye and Derrida. But they are less concerned with interpreting individual texts than with philosophizing about what literature may do and be; literary works are their occasion for the play of philosophical ideas about language. Many theorists do not regard practical interpretation as their chief aim. Indeed, some English departments have given up teaching poetry as a corpus of texts to be read, in favor of theoretical abstractions.

Theorists who spend more time philosophizing than reading a multitude of diverse texts are not the best guides to what is in literature. Biblical scholars who read theory with a narrow experience of literature as a whole are not qualified to judge how far a theory fits the observable facts. For example, Longman warns (53) that "secular theory . . . has united in its denial of any significance for the author." Theorists who say so exaggerate—and critics' *practice* is different. Many recent books on works of Shakespeare, Milton, and Spenser take the authors most seriously. Interpreters' practice is a better guide to the functions of literature than critical theories, and yet not the best guide available. Biblical scholars should rely less on models of critical praxis than on a broad firsthand acquaintance with the great variety of particular literary works. In centuries past, biblical interpreters have recognized the value of general literary experience. Lewis (1959, 154–57) urged the same point years prior to the rise of avowedly "literary" approaches to the parables. Unfortunately most of these approaches depend mainly on theory, rather than on the scholar's wide observation of literature in general. Biblical scholars sometimes show reluctance to appreciate the value of analogues in nonbiblical literature, regarding them as irrelevant to interpreting the Bible. The truth is that broad experience of secular literature is absolutely essential for a well-informed understanding of the text of a parable or of many other biblical texts.

Existing critical theories provide no adequate paradigm for the parables. Crossan's search for such a paradigm leads him to oversimplify Lewis's theory of "magistral" metaphors (simple tools of an author's preconceived thought) and "pupillary" metaphors (open-ended, exploratory means for an author's own fresh discoveries). Whereas Lewis says (1939, 140–41) that most metaphors lie between these extremes, Crossan arbitrarily identifies some of Jesus' parables as belonging to the pupillary extreme. The search for an adequate theoretical paradigm for the parables also leads structuralists such as Patte to force the parables into categories designed for a very different kind of story—one that does not have the sole purpose (as Jesus' parables do) of functioning in an analogy. In the same search Via adopts the theory that true literature is aesthetically autonomous from the real world, and applies it to texts most unsuited to it—since the main function of Jesus' parables, like that of all analogies, is to point beyond the artistically created world of fictional settings, characters, and events to the truth of the world in which we live.

The greatest exegetes of the parables—scholars such as Jeremias—cultivate a common-sense, inductive eclecticism. They have always used literary approaches (cf. parts 2 and 3), though often without the overt theorizing that distinguishes recent literary approaches to the parables. Yet they have not pursued inductive observation far enough to articulate the parables' essential workings as analogies. That is my purpose here. Most books on the parables (e.g., Jülicher, Hunter, Lambrecht, Stein) begin by developing a theory based on abstract and deductive arguments, before surveying the parables themselves. But throughout this book, inductive arguments draw on concrete examples from the Gospels to support the theory being developed here. Rather than adopting a literary point of view based on other literature, I emulate practical critics' *general* expectations of a text, asking: What is going on here? What is most important about these texts? What methods of study are therefore most suitable here? For the parables, my answer to the first two questions is "analogy" (Sider 1985). Thus part 1 uses examples from the parables and from classic parable interpretations to demonstrate how analogies work (with exercises to develop the student's practical skills of analysis); examples of analogies from nonbiblical texts emphasize that the logic of Jesus' analogies in the parables is pervasive in human language, from ordinary conversation to comic strips to Shakespeare.

Practical critics' *specific* expectations of a text concern how various components of literature typically operate: diction, style, plot, character, speeches, setting, point of view, tone, etc. The critic asks what characterizes their special operations in a given literary work. Part 2 allows students to practice interpreting parables in order to cultivate their expectations about how each aspect of a parable might work.

The purpose is similar in part 3, which deals with external factors that interpreters have always rightly regarded as relevant: the parables' cultural context, classification of literary kinds (genres), biblical context, and history of interpretation.

PARABLE AS ANALOGY

Culley (153–54) makes the excellent suggestion that in starting with the parables we should identify the essential minimum. That is, we should ask what is the least that is required for a text to be a parable at all. Culley regards that essential minimum as story. At the very least, however, the word *story* ordinarily denotes a narrative relation of one or more characters' actions elaborated enough to be called a "plot." The evangelists apply the word *parabole* to sayings of Jesus that are not stories even in a primitive sense, e.g., "Physician, heal yourself!" (Lk 4:23). Their usage of *parabole* corresponds to the common Greek usage of their time (quite apart from Greek rhetorical theory) as "analogy" whether story or not. Not all parables are stories, but every parable is an analogy (the logical form of the mathematical proportion below). If we start with this fact, our interpretation can be more clear, precise, and thorough. Mapping the logic of Jesus' analogies is essential to determining the significance of the parables' language, style, plot,

characters, etc. As many of my interpretive models show, interpreters have always dealt with the logic of analogy, though not
always systematically or with full awareness of the tacit principles
involved. (Thus Plato was teaching deductively before Aristotle
devised the syllogism to map his patterns of logic and test them.
For the parables, instead of the syllogism we need the simple formula of mathematical proportion: $A : B = a : b$.)

Understanding that all parables are analogies will dispel theoretical difficulties that have plagued scholars for a hundred years.
Jülicher began with analogy in 1888, invoking the proportional
formula $A : B = a : b$ (I, 69), and this century's parable studies
would look much different if his ill-conceived campaign against
allegorizing had not diverted him from his avowedly inductive
beginning. The "one-point theory"—his safeguard against allegorizing—prevented him from seeing how Jesus' parables generally
elaborate one proportional analogy into a series of related analogies. We shall see that if we extend a simple father-son comparison
(e.g., the Asking Son, Mt 7:9–11) into a full-fledged story (e.g.,
the Lost Son, Lk 15:11–32), one analogy is almost inevitably mul-
tiplied into several, and parable becomes allegory, every allegory
being an elaboration of analogy.

Rightly understood as "elaborated analogy," allegory is a
rhetorical device that may appear in any kind of literature (cf.
Boucher, 17). Often it appears only as an incidental feature in a literary work that is not allegorical overall (e.g., Sin and Death in
Milton's *Paradise Lost*, Book II). But when the device pervades a
work of literature (e.g., Bunyan's *Pilgrim's Progress*) we call it "an
allegorical work"—or, for short, "an allegory." The imprecision of
this latter phrase has misled many interpreters into thinking of
allegory as a separate literary genre or kind, rather than as a device
of rhetoric that never appears by itself as "an allegory," but always
as a feature in a literary genre that goes by some other name.
Strictly speaking, there are no "allegories," but only allegorical

stories such as *Pilgrim's Progress*, and allegorical dramas, proverbs, apocalypses, and so on.

Because allegory appears in literature of virtually all genres, its shapes are as diverse as all those literary kinds. Jülicher, however, ignores this variety, defining allegory as a separate genre with fixed characteristics: its form universally characterized by symbolism at every point of resemblance between image and theme and its content invariably marked by elements of the unrealistic or downright fantastic. In banishing allegorizing interpretation from the parables, Jülicher also banishes Jesus' allegorical intent by defining "parable" as the strict antithesis of "allegory"; having strictly realistic content and only one symbolic point of resemblance—no matter how elaborate the parable.

This false dichotomy between parable and allegory distorts scholars' perceptions of literary allegory. For example, when Bunyan's Christian encounters a parlor too dusty to be swept until it has been watered, of course we need to have the symbolism explained. But it is wrong for Jones (89) to use this rather unusual case to argue that allegory is typically incomprehensible without a key. For we have just met a new character, Interpreter, and Bunyan supplies a mystery to demonstrate his powers: "The parlour is the heart of a man...." Like any other classic of the common reader, *Pilgrim's Progress* is as perspicuous as the Bible. Except for a false theory of allegory, no scholar would say otherwise.

Despite the recent work of Boucher and Blomberg, the false dichotomy also creates distorted interpretations of the parables. Many exegetes deny, with Dodd, that a parable such as the Sower has any allegorical content because it is realistic, as Jeremias (128) says the Lost Son "is not an allegory, but a story drawn from life." They conclude that the Sower has but one point, and that the elaborate synoptic interpretation must be an imposition of the evangelists or their sources. Using this reasoning one could say that because Paul's allegory of the body of Christ (1Co 12:14–21) unrealistically makes bodily members speak, he must therefore intend a separate symbolism for each member that he mentions—foot, hand, ear, eye—though obviously he makes just one point: The welfare of the whole depends on each part. Conversely, one could as well argue that because many episodes of Spenser's *Faerie Queene* are perfectly realistic (e.g., I.vii.1–7.3, II.i.1–34, III.ix.1–x.17), they have only one symbolic point—though all of them have more, and some dozens. Modern interpreters who, with Stein, still resist "pressing the details" tend to summarize a complex parable in language that purports to make only one point but actually conveys more. Though Jeremias says that only four parables make as many as two points, he unwittingly articulates eight in the brief parable of the Growing Seed, as we shall see, and more in the Unmerciful Servant. An objective survey of the rhetoric of allegory in general (including the Bible) shows that the symbolic points may be many or few.

Jülicher did not need the one-point theory. Allegorizing interpretations were based on a sacramental view of all of Scripture, which from patristic times was interpreted just as allegorically as the parables. He could have attacked allegorical exegesis in general while freely acknowledging the complex figurative symbolism of the parables. (For more details of his theory see appendix A.)

Some interpreters are uneasy about limiting a parable to one point but still regard that as the only justifiable alternative to the unlicensed and arbitrary allegorizing of every detail. If we admit more than one symbolic point, they ask, is it not arbitrary to draw a line short of pervasive symbolism? Without arbitrariness secular interpretation draws the line between the legitimate allegorical reading of symbolic details and the unlicensed allegorization of details that have only literal significance. But one cannot draw the line by any simple rule such as Blomberg's. (He suggests limiting the points of a parable to the number of its central characters, but this oversimplifies matters; his wording often comprises several points in what purports to be one.) *The topics in parts 2 and 3 comprise a network of complementary cues, such as are used to delimit symbolism in secular literature, that can give us reasonable assurance about which features of a parable are figurative symbols and which are only literal and incidental details.*

Such cues guide the very first exegesis of Jesus' parable of the Tenants, when the Jewish leaders perceive that he has "told the parable against them" (Mk 12:12). Here Jesus elaborates an analogy into a complex allegory. How do they detect the symbolic correspondence of the vineyard tenants with themselves? Several diverse cues point them in the right direction. First, the *situation* of their confrontation with Jesus makes them expect some rejoinder. They have challenged him directly (Mk 11:28): "By what authority are you doing these things?" He has refused to answer, but they may well expect this tragic story to carry an oblique reply. Second, the *traditional symbols* in the initial description of the vineyard clearly identify the Jewish authorities' place in the analogy. Jesus' first words virtually quote Isaiah 5:1–2, and 5:7 says: "The vineyard of the Lord Almighty is the house of Israel." The tenant farmers who are entrusted with its care must be the chief priests, scribes, and elders. Third, the *structure* of the analogy clarifies some details. The basic symbolic correspondences point to others: the servants must be the prophets, and their mistreatment must be the authorities' contempt for the prophetic word. (These men have just rejected John the Baptist's divine authority.) And Jesus so plainly indicates their motive for his own death (first broached as early as Mk 3:6) that they may recognize him as the owner's son. Fourth, to remove all doubt Jesus' *commentary* claims his prime place in God's scheme, despite opposition (Mk 12:10): "The stone the builders rejected has become the capstone." The authorities got Jesus' point—they wanted to arrest him.

But these original hearers may have missed some important points. One servant was struck on the head—perhaps in allusion to the beheading of John. The phrase "son, whom he loved" may be a reminder of the voice from heaven at Jesus' baptism (Mk 1:11). "They ... threw him out of the vineyard" could refer to Jesus' crucifixion outside Jerusalem (Jn 19:20). What of "the inheritance will be ours" (12:7)? Is this symbolic too, or just a motive to keep the plot going? To answer such questions a thorough and responsible interpreter will use all the available cues, including the features that guided the Jewish leaders' interpretation: internal features such as *structure* and *commentary* (part 2) and external features such as *situation* and *traditional symbols* (part 3).

Only by a thorough analysis of the parables' logic of analogy—epitomized in the simple formula A : B = a : b, but often intricate and unpredictably various—can we grasp the full scope of what they *might* mean. And only by a systematic survey of their other features can we subsequently determine, as far as possible, what they *do* mean.

INTERPRETING THE PARABLES AS ANALOGIES

From the praxis of this book emerges a working theory to be tested and confirmed or modified by the reader's own experience. This is the method of my Literary Analysis course at Westmont College, in which I address various interpretive techniques and help students analyze the practice of an established critic in an extract of published criticism that models each technique. Then I critique students' experiments with the technique in a preliminary exercise and have them write a formal interpretive essay that puts the technique to work.

This book guides readers through a cumulative sequence of practical exercises in the wide range of basic techniques that biblical scholars have shown to be valuable for the parables. Almost every topic is introduced by precedents drawn from existing exegesis, the "Interpretive Models," followed by my analysis to help readers appreciate the scholars' methods. The practical exercises are directed primarily at students who use the book as a course text: to encourage them to experiment with the methods and to do what all good critics do—improve on such models and precedents however they can. The conclusion of the book encourages readers to integrate the various methods.

The interpretive models reflect divergent beliefs about what a parable is and how it works. Each is chosen to be useful, not necessarily to epitomize or endorse its author's whole work. Not all of these scholars would endorse every inference that I draw from their work, or approve of all the company they keep in this book. The models show something else incidentally: *the practice of responsible exegetes already contains, mostly in tacit form, the whole basis of a literary theory more complete and coherent than any that has yet been articulated for the parables.* That is, there is little in this book that is new to scholars' practice of interpreting the parables but much that has not been systematically described hitherto.

The models are extracted from well-known studies, but my description of the tacit theory that underlies them may be unfamiliar. Part 1 is not exactly a "quick read." Spending time on the exercises may be the most important thing. As in mathematics, we are dealing with logical processes, and exercises are the best way to make them reflexive. To absorb algebra most of us need to do more than passively watch the teacher do equations; likewise the exercises on the parables will help develop practical skills as well as a literary theory of the parables. Some ideas will be readily clear; but if more exercises are needed for other concepts, the questions provided can be easily applied to other parables.

This book asks questions that can benefit those who have no specialized literary training. That means excluding structuralist and deconstructionist approaches, as well as Freudian, Marxist, feminist, and existentialist readings, and any other approach that is too much like one-issue politics. Students need ample experience of practical criticism before they can discern whether a theory holds a mirror up to the nature of many parables, a few, or none at all. The nuts-and-bolts concepts and techniques of practical criticism are essential (with varying applications) to any of the specialized theories just mentioned. For the history of parable interpretation see Kissinger and Blomberg.

Most recent scholars have tried to trace the traditions of Jesus' sayings that lie behind the texts of our Gospels and to distinguish between his very own words (his *ipsissima verba*, as they are called) and the evangelists' renditions of the parables as they may have been altered in the decades between Jesus' ministry and the writing of the Gospels. But this book makes no attempt of that kind. One reason is that Blomberg makes a strong argument for the essential authenticity of the parables in the gospel texts. Another reason, conclusive by itself, is that the results of reconstructing scholarship are a much inferior evidence, the "original" version of Jesus' words depending largely on whose scholarship one reads. The variously conjectured ending-points of the Unjust Judge (Lk 18:1–8) are a celebrated case, not an isolated one. Scholars cannot agree about which features of the Gospel texts are secondary additions to Jesus' original words, because they must use many hypotheses with a degree of probability that is indifferent at best, leading to conclusions that in logic must be much less probable (Sider 1983). And all such reconstructions depend on various mistaken or premature literary ideas. Jeremias's work, for example, is fatally flawed by a cluster of assumptions now increasingly recognized as untenable (thus Blomberg, 29–69): that allegory and parable do not mix, that Jesus seldom if ever used allegory, and therefore that most allegorical elements in the gospel versions of the parables are secondary additions. Other literary assumptions are superficial and thus premature. *No one has yet given the parables in their gospel versions a sufficiently thorough literary analysis to justify the literary judgments by which interpreters typically detect the activity of the evangelists or their informants*. In the Good Samaritan, for example (Lk 10:25–37), "The disjunction between question and answer, considered so grievous by Jülicher and those who have followed him, far from being inimical to the parable, is necessary to the point" (Funk 1966, 221). The more one learns about the literary features of the parables in their gospel form, the more ambiguous appears the evidence that supports any divergent reconstruction of Jesus' "actual words." According to Norman Perrin (1976, 101), "When we talk of interpreting the parables of Jesus today we mean interpreting the parables as Jeremias has reconstructed them, either personally or through his influence on others who have followed the method he developed." But in the present state of knowledge the versions of the parables in the canonical Gospels bring us about as close to the "parables of Jesus" as we can come. (The significance of the parables in the Gospel of Thomas is uncertain because of a similar lack of consensus in scholarly speculations about their origins and evolution.) Thus a more precise title for this book would be "Interpreting the Parables *of the Jesus of the Four Gospels*."

PART
I

The Structure of Argument in the Parables

Because analogy is what makes a parable a parable, we must analyze the typical *form* of Jesus' analogies, which is proportional comparison, and their invariable *content*, which is argument. We begin with the simplest analogies, and proceed to various kinds of elaboration—finding ample evidence along the way to show that elaborated analogy naturally becomes allegorical.

1

PROPORTIONAL COMPARISONS

The logic of Jesus' brief parabolic sayings is *proportional analogy*, as Jülicher noted (I, 69). His interpretation of the Unworthy Servants (Lk 17:7–10) articulates the proportional comparison in the parable.

INTERPRETIVE MODEL

Jülicher, II, 16–18 (auth. tr.)

> A disciple's relationship to God is being compared with that of a slave to his master. In the latter case it is obviously clear that the slave does all his duties without demanding thanks; and the same principle applies as the sole standard for spiritual life also. . . .
>
> Jesus is urging his disciples that even the best person can never do more than his duty—that he may claim thanks from God just as little as an unfailingly diligent slave might from his master.

Jülicher's analysis exemplifies two essential steps in interpreting any parable. First he identifies the two things that the analogy compares. Jesus' theme, the *tenor* of the parable (Ger. *Sache*), is "a disciple's relationship to God"; his pictorial image, the *vehicle* of the parable (Ger. *Bild*), is "that of a slave to his master." (Some

29

scholars have called these two parts of Jesus' comparisons the "reality part" and the "picture part"; *tenor* and *vehicle* are the usual terms in secular criticism.) Here is the proportional form of these analogous terms.

TENOR		VEHICLE
disciple : God	=	slave : master

That is: The disciple is to God as the slave is to the master. This is the logic of similes and metaphors in general. Levin (13) notes it in *Macbeth*, 1.7.25–28: "I have no spur / To prick the sides of my intent, but only / Vaulting ambition."

TENOR		VEHICLE
ambition : intention	=	spur : [horse]

Second, Jülicher identifies the *point of resemblance:* "Even the best person can never do more than his duty." How can he know which of the possible similarities between disciples and slaves is the key to Jesus' meaning? The cue is the final comment of the parable: "So you also, when you have done everything you were told to do, should say, 'We are unworthy servants; we have only done our duty.'" To express this point of resemblance, we add a second line to the formula.

TENOR		VEHICLE
disciple : God	=	slave : master
with respect to unsurpassable obligation		
POINT OF RESEMBLANCE		

This is the only formula we need to map the logic of all the parables except a few "example-stories": the Good Samaritan (Lk 10:25–37), the Pharisee and Publican (Lk 18:9–14), the Rich Fool (Lk 12:13–21), and the Rich Man and Lazarus (Lk 16:19–31) (Sider 1981). Some scholars call the point of resemblance the *ter-*

tium comparationis—Latin for "third [term] of the comparison," the tenor and vehicle being the first and second terms.

As in any analogy, Jesus proceeds from the known to the unknown. Thus the Physician for the Sick (Mk 2:16–17).

INTERPRETIVE MODEL

Hunter, 52

> When the Scribes asked why he consorted with "publicans and sinners"—with notoriously bad men and women and folk who followed dishonourable or immoral professions—Jesus replied: "It is not the healthy who need the doctor but the sick (Don't you understand why I gather these outcasts into my company? They are ill and need help!). For I did not come," he adds in one of those sayings in which the secret of his presence in the world is disclosed, "to call righteous men but sinners."

Hunter does not have to say, in Jülicher's fashion, "The outcasts' relationship to Jesus is being compared with a sick person's to a physician." His readers already grasp the analogy. But Jesus' words imply that outcasts are to Jesus as the sick are to a physician.

TENOR	VEHICLE
outcasts : Jesus = sick : physician	
with respect to the need for help	
POINT OF RESEMBLANCE	

The following Shakespearean analogies closely resemble this proportional form. The first describes an amateur actor murdering his lines; the second expresses our subordination to God's purposes; the third needs no explanation.

(1)

TENOR		VEHICLE
"He hath played on this prologue	like	a child on a recorder—
a sound, but not in government."		
POINT OF RESEMBLANCE		*A Midsummer Night's Dream* 5.1.122–24

TENOR   VEHICLE

inept player saying prologue : his lines = untutored child : recorder

    with respect to creating incoherent noise

POINT OF RESEMBLANCE

(2)

TENOR		VEHICLE
"Heaven doth with us	as	we with torches do,
Not light them for themselves."		
POINT OF RESEMBLANCE		*Measure for Measure* 1.1.32–33

TENOR   VEHICLE

God : humans = humans : torches

    with respect to ulterior purposes

POINT OF RESEMBLANCE

(3)

VEHICLE		TENOR
"As flies to wanton boys	are	we to th' gods:
They kill us for their sport."		
POINT OF RESEMBLANCE		*King Lear* 4.1.36–37

TENOR   VEHICLE

humans : gods = flies : wanton boys

    with respect to pleasure taken in deadly suffering

POINT OF RESEMBLANCE

In example (3), except for the inversion of grammatical subject and complement, Shakespeare's language is identical to the way we read the proportion: "We are to the gods as flies are to wanton boys." But the *underlying logic* of analogy is expressed in many forms of *surface rhetoric* that hardly ever look like this proportional statement of Shakespeare's. Examples (1) and (2) are somewhat divergent, and the texts of most analogies—including the Unworthy Servants and the Physician for the Sick—diverge much farther from the formula.

In the Physician for the Sick Jesus' meaning is so simple and obvious that we may not need the formula to evaluate Hunter's interpretation, but many parables are not so straightforward. For example, interpreters may agree on what constitutes the basic analogy of the Sower (Mk 4:3–8) but disagree about the point of resemblance. Mowry (I, 84; III, 652) calls the parable "a calm observation that misfortunes are unavoidable," for "as the farmer must expect varying returns from his activity, so God also at the time of judgment." Henry (V, 470) emphasizes the good and bad: "The word of God is dispensed to all promiscuously," as God sends rain on the just and the unjust. Wilson (804) says that Mark's interpretation stresses the alternative responses, and hence "the responsibility of the hearers." Montefiore (I, 100) finds the main point in the fact that the seed grows rapidly on rocky and thorny ground, but good fruit takes longer; the parable therefore suggests not imminent eschatology but "the gradual reception of [Jesus'] teaching by a dull and reluctant world." In such a case the proportional formula can help us clarify these interpreters' divergences and determine which reading(s) may be preferable.

TENOR   VEHICLE
receptive hearers : unreceptive hearers = seed in good soil :
    seed in bad soil
with respect to (1) difference in quantity (Mowry)

(2) difference in quality (Henry)
(3) difference in response (Wilson on Mark)
(4) difference in timing (Montefiore)
POINTS OF RESEMBLANCE

Except for the handful of example-stories already mentioned, all of Jesus' parables contain this logic of proportional comparison. In the Thief (Lk 12:39–40; cf. Mt 24:43–44) we find Jesus' *vehicle* (the pictorial image) in verse 39: "The owner of the house [did not know] at what hour the thief was coming". His *tenor* (the theme) is expressed in verse 40: "You [do not know when] the Son of Man will come," as well as the *point of resemblance:* "Be ready."

TENOR	VEHICLE
disciples: coming of the Son of man	= householder :
	coming of the thief

with respect to readiness for the unexpected
POINT OF RESEMBLANCE

For another useful interpretive model see Heard (63–64) on the Unjust Steward (Lk 16:1–13).

EXERCISE

Exercises on the Budding Fig Tree (Mk 13:28–29) and the Unmerciful Servant (Mt 18:23–35)

1. Articulate the essential meaning of the "'lesson' from the fig tree" (Mk 13:28; "analogy" is a better translation for *parabole* than "lesson") by expressing its tenor and vehicle in the four terms of a mathematical proportion, with a second line for the point of resemblance, as in the examples above. Place the two terms of the tenor first (on the left), making Jesus' theme the first part of your grammatical subject, and place the two terms of the vehicle last (on the right). There is always more than one way to "translate" Jesus' parables into these structured

terms of analogy. It helps to experiment with different possibilities; after trying your own expression of the formula, compare the one on p. 189.

2. The longest of Jesus' stories make proportional analogies,
    sometimes more than one. Using the same format of propor-
    tion, articulate the analogy that expresses the main point of
    the Unmerciful Servant. Compare your result with the for-
    mula on p. 69.

Wording the formula carefully can help us determine what
the text means. In its final form, however, one's exegetical commentary on a parable is better conveyed in language less mechanical and more presentable to a reader, such as Jülicher's and
Hunter's comments quoted above. Formulating a proportion is just
the beginning, of course. We shall ask many other questions that
may modify the statement of the basic analogy.

With every parable, from simple statement to elaborate story,
one should begin by identifying this basic analogy. Jesus' longest
parables are just like the short similitudes of the Unworthy Servants and the Physician for the Sick, in that the main point consists of a proportional analogy. He uses many forms of *speech* in his
parables—such as questions, stories, and proverbs—but these
diverse expressions embody just one form of *thought*. Analogy is
the chief literary feature common to the sayings called *parabolai*.
Nothing else about them justifies making one genre of such diverse
materials: from the three-word proverb of Luke 4:23 to the
twenty-two-verse story of the Lost Son (Lk 15:11–32). A saying
of Jesus is a "parable" not because it expresses or implies a story,
but because it involves a comparison by analogy.

2

RHETORICAL ELLIPSIS

Unlike the three Shakespearean examples above, Jesus' language in the parables never spells out a proportional formula in so many words. He does not say: "You disciples are to the coming of the Son of man as the householder is to the thief: readiness for the unexpected is necessary." Most parables have some *ellipsis* (omission) of terms. Part of the analogy is only implied.

ELLIPSIS OF TENOR

In the parable of the Unworthy Servants Jesus' words denote only half the tenor (Lk 17:10): "So you also . . . should say, 'We are unworthy servants, we have only done our duty.'" He could have supplied the rest of the tenor by saying "unworthy servants *of God*," but the implication is clear enough.

> the disciple : [God]   =   a slave : his master
> with respect to unsurpassable obligation

So too with the parable of the Tenants (Mk 12:1–12; cf. Mt 21:33–46; Lk 20:9–19): though Jesus never names the tenor, the chief priests, the teachers of the law, and the elders all "knew he had spoken the parable against them" (Mk 12:12).

> [leaders of Israel: God]   =   tenants : vineyard owner
> with respect to crime and punishment

Compare Orwell's novel *Animal Farm,* which never mentions his tenor, and yet his special combination of "characters" and situations can only point to Russia in revolution. The context of a conversation also may explain the tenor well enough. When asked, "Why don't the Beatles reunite?" Paul McCartney could answer, "You can't reheat a souffle," and not have to spell out the correspondences between his image and the tenor of the question.

Upon hearing the story of the Sower, however, the disciples could not fill in the tenor of the analogy for themselves (Mk 4:10): "When he was alone, the Twelve and the others around him asked him about the parables." To explain the Sower, Jesus matched vehicle and tenor (4:14): "The farmer sows the word...."

> [preacher] : word   =   farmer : seed
> with respect to divergent reception by various soils, etc.

The texts of the Leaven (Mt 13:33; Lk 13:20–21) do not make the whole tenor explicit; we must infer part of it.

INTERPRETIVE MODEL

Kistemaker, 50

> The point of the parable is that the yeast, once added to the flour, permeates the entire batch of dough until every particle is affected. The yeast is hidden from sight, and yet its effect is visible to all. That is how the kingdom of God demonstrates its power and presence in today's world.

All of the essentials in this interpretation are explicit in the gospel text except one: the "world." Different interpreters have completed the analogy in different ways; given the terms of the image, and what the Gospels say about the kingdom, Kistemaker makes a good choice.

kingdom : [the world]   =   yeast : dough
with respect to pervasiveness

Often we mentally "fill in the blanks" in the parables without thinking about our choices. This sort of thing can happen in the ordinary *reading* of any text, when one's state of mind is spontaneous, imaginative, and largely unreflective. But the process of *interpreting* a text must be a retrospective follow-up to the simple reading of it. In this second stage one tries to discover the ways in which the initial reading was less than ideal. What did we inadvertently misunderstand or overlook? What did we mistakenly read into the text? Though this second process must be still partly spontaneous and imaginative, it is much more calculating, self-conscious, and rational than just "reading."

Thus, for example, in the simple reading of a parable we spontaneously intuit the structure of the analogy. But to find out if our intuitions are correct and complete, we need to look back upon that experience of *reading*, by adopting the more reflective mode, *interpretation*. In this second process the place to begin is with a precisely worded formula of proportion. This schematization makes it easier to detect the tacit choices that we made while intuitively identifying the terms of Jesus' analogy—and supplying any elliptical terms by "reading between the lines." The formula also helps us account responsibly for possibilities that may not have come to mind in the spontaneous act of reading.

Let us try the formula on a second reading of the Leaven.

INTERPRETIVE MODEL

Jeremias, 148–49

We are shown a tiny morsel of leaven..., absurdly small in comparison with the great mass of more than a bushel of meal. The housewife mixes it, covers it with a cloth, leaves the mass to stand overnight, and when she returns to it in the morning the whole mass of dough is leavened.... [Jesus says:] "With the same compelling certainty that causes ... a small piece of leaven to produce a vast mass of dough, will God's miraculous power cause my small band to swell into the mighty host of the people of God in the Messianic Age, embracing the Gentiles."

Instead of using Jesus' phrase "the kingdom" to express the tenor, Jeremias specifies two features of the kingdom—the first disciples and the whole company of the faithful. For the point of resemblance he chooses a different feature of the vehicle: the contrast between beginning and completion.

[small band] : [mighty host]   =   [morsel of] yeast :
    [mass of] dough
[with respect to spectacular growth over time]

The formula dramatizes how much more Jeremias has inferred from the text. Since Kistemaker's interpretation of "pervasiveness" is authorized by the text's "all through the dough," can Jeremias justify reading the contrast of size between the lines? We should not just assume that the best interpretation adds least to the text. For if Jesus had Jeremias's point in mind, he might well use the exact words found in Matthew or Luke.

In many parables such as the one about the Leaven, two or more plausible readings emerge. That is why a thorough interpretation must include all the features of a parable that are addressed in parts 2 and 3. Any feature could dictate which version of an analogy is most appropriate or how many versions are parts of Jesus' meaning. Jeremias justifies his reading of this parable by invoking two of these features. One is the parable's *affinity with other parables* (see part 3.3), in this case, the Mustard Seed. It is the very smallest thing the human eye can perceive (148):

> Every word [of Mark 4:31b] emphasizes its smallness—and when it is grown, it is "the greatest among all the herbs, and puts forth great branches, so that the birds of heaven make their nests in its shadow" (v. 32)—every word depicts the size of the shrub, which, by the Lake of Gennessaret, attains a height of about 8 to 10 feet.

Jeremias infers that the contrast of size, explicit in the Mustard Seed, is the point of the Leaven too. The second feature appeals to *traditional symbols* (see part 3.1): "The tree which shelters the birds is a common metaphor for a mighty kingdom which protects its vassals, and the dough in Rom. 11.16 is a metaphor for the people of God" (147). By showing that Jesus' images of the dough and of the tree sheltering birds have customary symbolic value denoting large groups of people, Jeremias offers some justification for seeing the tenor as "small band" and "mighty host," rather than as simply "kingdom," as Kistemaker suggests.

The text of the Barren Fig Tree (Lk 13:6–9) gives only the vehicle of Jesus' analogy. This one is a very short story which, like all of his vehicles, creates the concrete pictorial effect that we call an *image*. In this case we must infer the whole of his tenor.

INTERPRETIVE MODEL

Blomberg, 268–69

> The vineyard was a stock metaphor for Israel, so it is natural to take the fig tree here as representing at least some of the Jews. Their fruitlessness is self-explanatory. In light of Jesus' special condemnation of the corrupt leadership of the Jewish nation elsewhere, the fig tree would naturally symbolize the religious leaders of Israel, though the principle of judgment on those who do not repent obviously applies universally.

Blomberg identifies all the elements of the basic analogy:

    God : corrupt Jewish leaders   =   vineyard owner : barren
        fig tree
    with respect to the imminence of destruction

In order to read the symbols, Blomberg relies on two cues that are external to the parable: other parts of the New Testament (for Jesus' condemnation of the Jewish leaders), and an Old Testament tradition (for the vineyard as Israel). See Blomberg for more interpretive models, e.g., pp. 247–51 on the Tenants.

EXERCISE

Exercise on the Children in the Marketplace (Mt 11:16–19; Lk 7:31–35)
    Supply the elliptical tenor by using the same two-line formula. Which of Jesus' words should one choose for use as the four terms of the proportion? Which terms are implied and need to be supplied? In choosing your terms pay careful attention to the prior context (Mt 11:1ff.; Lk 7:18ff.). Compare the formulas on p. 128.

ELLIPSIS OF THE POINT OF RESEMBLANCE

    Some parable texts specify both tenor and vehicle, but not the point of resemblance. They may be hard to interpret if more than one feature of the vehicle could be the point of resemblance, as in the following situation.

By permission of Jonnny Hart and Creators Syndicate, Inc.

glasses : Clumsy   =   wooden leg : Wiley
with respect to (1) usefulness for carrying booze
or (2) necessity for ordinary physical functions

Just as Clumsy does not say *how* his glasses are like Wiley's
wooden leg, so Jesus does not tell us in what respect the image of
the Householders' Treasure (Mt 13:51–52) is like the kingdom; he
just says it is. What then is the key point?

INTERPRETIVE MODEL

Hunter, 65–66

> Perhaps the little parable of The Householder was
> [Jesus'] answer to a Scribe who had volunteered his
> allegiance but wondered whether what he had learned
> 'under the Law' would be useless in the high emprise of
> the Kingdom. . . .
>
> A Scribe who becomes my disciple, says Jesus, will
> be able to wed the wisdoms of the Old Order to the
> truths of the New.

For Hunter the point is neither the householder nor the treasure.
Perhaps taking his cue from the Patched Garment and the Wineskins (Mk 2:21–22; Mt 9:16–17; Lk 5:36–38), he focuses on this
parable's stated contrast between new and old.

old [order's wisdom] : new [order's truths] = old treasure :
        new treasure

In what respect does this image resemble the kingdom? Hunter
must make an educated guess.

old [order's wisdom] : new [order's truths] = old treasure :
        new treasure
[with respect to compatibility]

The old and new treasures resemble the old and new order in other respects: they are very valuable, they are easily accessible, etc. What prompts Hunter's choice? One good reason is the context (see part 3.3) of Matthew's emphasis on this theme (e.g., 5:17–20): "Do not think that I have come to abolish the Law or the Prophets; I have not come to abolish them but to fulfill them." See also Stein (94–95) on the Mustard Seed and the Leaven (Mt 13:31–33; Mk 4:30–32; Lk 13:18–21).

EXERCISE

Exercise on the Wise Builder (Mt 7:24–25)

Clearly Jesus is saying in this parable: "Obey my words as well as hearing them." But what is it about a wise builder that specially suits his theme? (This will be the point of resemblance.) Use the analogy formula to represent Jesus' meaning, reading additional terms between the lines as necessary. You may find more possibilities than you can use; note the justification for your choices. Compare the formula on p. 144.

3

VARIETIES OF COMPARISON

The logic of Jesus' comparisons in parable sometimes looks different from the analogies that we have been analyzing. In each of those, the comparison is a matter of simple equation, but in some parables the comparison is not of two equal things, and sometimes it is actually a contrast.

A FORTIORI ARGUMENTS

Most of Jesus' comparisons assert equality, but others, such as the Asking Son (Mt 7:9–11; Lk 11:11–13) contrast the greater and the less.

INTERPRETIVE MODEL

Hunter, 68

> The argument is: "No ordinary human father—and the best of them are far from perfect—would play a scurvy trick like this on his son. How much less then the good Father above!"

Hunter does not mean that the likelihood of such a "scurvy trick" is the same for God as for a human father, but that, for God, the likelihood is much smaller. To put his interpretation in our proportional terms, the phrase we need is not "is equal to" (=), but rather "is less than" (<).

our all-good God : [those who ask]   <   "evil" father : ask-
    ing son
with respect to the likelihood of an ungracious response

Jesus exclaims, "How much more . . . !" Where does Hunter
find "How much less . . ." in the parable? What the image depicts
is not a human father's graciousness, but two scurvy tricks, and
Hunter expresses what the explicit image of human unkindness
suggests about God. But Jesus' rhetorical question clearly implies
that the ordinary human father would respond with generosity to
his child's request, and his commentary expresses what this implied
image of human kindness suggests about God.

[our all-good] God : those who ask   >   "evil" father : ask-
    ing children
with respect to graciousness of response

Jesus' image puts it one way and his commentary puts it the other;
Hunter's acute exegesis includes both. The main point ("God is
good" or "God answers prayer") is dually conveyed by complementary *a fortiori* comparisons—the positive one is explicit and
the negative one is implied in the image.

God's care for humans is even more trustworthy than his
obvious care for the ravens and lilies (Mt 6:25–30; Lk 12:22–28)
and the sparrows (Mt 10:29–31; Lk 12:6–7), or than the courtesy
of the Friend at Midnight (Lk 11:5–8)—three good subjects for
practical exercise with *a fortiori* argument. We can hardly make
analogies about God without some sense of "how much more."

EXERCISE

Exercise on the Unjust Steward (Lk 16:1–13)

For this parable construct separate proportional formulas to
express at least two unequal comparisons using ">" and "<" to inter-

pret verses 8 and 11. Compare the formula on p. 152. The Maligned Master (Mt 10:24–25) is a good subject for more practice.

NEGATIVE COMPARISONS

When Jesus' analogy depends on a contrast rather than a similarity, the negative comparison requires special treatment. The point of the Weather Signs (Lk 12:54–56) is a contrast.

INTERPRETIVE MODEL

Hunter, 76

> "You men of Israel," says Jesus, "have merely to glance at the sky or note the wind's direction, and you can tell the weather. But God is visiting his people in blessing and judgment, and you can't see it."

Hunter skillfully captures the working of this rather unusual analogy, whose equation is not positive, but negative.

signs of the times : God's visitation ≠ weather signs : weather

with respect to the obviousness of the connection

Compare Isaiah's analogy of a forgetful mother (49:14–15): "But Zion said, 'The Lord has forsaken me, the Lord has forgotten me.' 'Can a mother forget the baby at her breast and have no compassion on the child she has borne? Though she may forget, I will not forget you!'"

God : Zion ≠ forgetful mother : child

with respect to neglect

So too the Foxes and Birds (Mt 8:19–20; Lk 9:57–58), Clean and Unclean (Mk 7:17–23; Mt 15:10–20), and the Old and New Wine (Lk 5:39; cf. Jeremias, 104 n.70).

(1) Jesus   ≠   foxes and birds
with respect to possession of a home

(2) evil thoughts: heart   ≠   ceremonially unclean food
   : stomach
with respect to defilement

(3a) man : old wine   =   Jews : Old Age
with respect to appreciation

(3b) old wine : new wine   ≠   Old Age : New Age
with respect to actual relative value

One routine interpretive step is to look for aspects of Jesus' message that are conveyed by negative comparisons. Just at the point where an analogy breaks down, an ingenious author may exploit the difference as well as the similarity.

EXERCISE

Exercise on Unjust Judge (Lk 18:1–8)

Construct a formula to express the negative comparison in the Unjust Judge. Is Jesus' main point a positive comparison, negative, or *a fortiori?*

4

ANALOGY CLUSTERS

Two or more analogies may work together in the discourse of Jesus' preaching or conversation. When two or three successive analogies make the same basic point (e.g., the Lost Sheep, Coin, and Son in Luke 15), we may speak of a *doublet* or *triplet* (cf. part 1.6). In other cases analogies in series can convey separate steps of Jesus' argument. Such a *sequence* may be either *discursive* or *narrative*.

DISCURSIVE SEQUENCES

Sometimes it appears that Jesus composed a whole discourse out of analogies, either in the main (e.g., large stretches of the Sermon on the Mount) or entirely—as on one occasion when Mark observes that Jesus "did not say anything to them without using a parable" (4:34). The whole discourse of Mark 4 consists of analogies: the Sower, the Lamp on a Stand, the Growing Seed, and the Mustard Seed. Here Mark makes "parable" include brief analogies like the Lamp on a Stand. Large stretches of the Sermon on the Mount and other discourses are parabolic too.

Successive images sometimes seem like mixed metaphors (e.g., Mt 7:15–16): "Watch out for false prophets. They come to you in sheep's clothing, but inwardly they are ferocious wolves. By their fruit you will recognize them." Clearly we are meant to hold the two images in mind distinctly and sequentially.

(1) false prophets' appearance : true nature   =   sheep's
    clothing : wolves
with respect to danger of deception

(2) false prophets : their effects = bad tree : bad fruit
with respect to evidence of true nature

Even sudden transitions can be so smooth that the reader's spontaneous response is not distracted at all; thus Hamlet's "take arms
against a sea." Macbeth's metaphorical analogy represents ambition two different ways in the same verbal picture.

> I have no spur
> To prick the sides of my intent, but only
> Vaulting ambition, which o'erleaps itself,
> And falls on th' other.

(1) ambition : intention = spur : [horse]
(2) ambition : intention = [rider : horse]

Likewise, Jesus compares himself first with the gate of the fold and
then with the shepherd of the sheep, in a single piece of discourse
(Jn 10:7ff.).

A pair of analogies such as the Divided Kingdom and the
Strong Man Bound (Mk 3:22–27; Mt 12:24–29; Lk 11:15–22)
can convey related points.

INTERPRETIVE MODEL

Hunter, 48–49

Both these parables were born in the cut-and-thrust
of that campaign in which Jesus not only proclaimed
the presence of the Kingdom but in its name delivered
men and women from demons and disease, so that he
drew down on himself the charge of being in league
with the powers of darkness. In the first parable he says
in effect: "Collusion with the arch-fiend, you say? But

> dog does not eat dog. The true interpretation of the facts is that the devil's realm, being divided, is doomed." He makes a like point in The Strong Man Bound where his wording very significantly echoes Isa. 49.24f. (a Servant passage). It is the Servant Messiah who speaks: "My exorcisms show that I am the devil's master. The captives of the mighty, as Isaiah foretold, are being taken and the prey of the tyrant rescued."

The Divided Kingdom focuses on what Jesus' exorcisms say about the evil one: if Satan really is fighting himself, then his power is broken.

> Satan casting out demons : Satan's rule = civil war : a kingdom
> with respect to evidence of disintegration

The Strong Man Bound, however, focuses on what Jesus' exorcisms say about himself.

> Jesus : Satan's kingdom = plunderer : a strong man's house
> with respect to control

Whose power is casting out demons—Satan's or Jesus'? Either way, the devil's tyranny is ending.

Adjacent analogies in Jesus' discourse are nearly always linked by theme; therefore a thorough study of one image must reckon with its neighbors. Although texts in Mark and Luke contain a third image—the Divided House—and Matthew includes a fourth—the Divided City—Hunter gives these alternate images no separate notice, probably because they so closely resemble the Divided Kingdom.

> Satan casting out demons : Satan's rule = domestic division : a family
> with respect to evidence of disintegration

Satan casting out demons : Satan's rule = municipal strife :
   a city
with respect to evidence of disintegration

The additional images dispel any doubt about the point of the first one. They also reinforce it by showing that it is not an isolated case. Jesus' point, "Divided we fall," is a general principle that we could demonstrate by a host of examples. This is one function of *doublets* (part 1.6).

The Salt of the Earth, the Light of the World, the City on a Hill, and the Lamp on a Lampstand (Mt 5:13–16) comprise a longer series of related analogies.

INTERPRETIVE MODEL

Ridderbos, 94–95

What [Jesus] had in mind here is the preservative power of salt. By "earth" He meant human society and, beyond this, the whole world as the setting for life. Jesus' disciples thus have a preservative influence on human society, and through it on all other things. They counteract the corruption and decay that is at work in the world. . . .

Jesus uses another image, that of light, to describe His disciples' significance and task in the world. As verse 16 makes clear, this light is visible in their good works. Such works point the way to those living in darkness and also give them inspiration and joy. . . .

Believers cannot fail to exert such a wholesome influence on the world around them. Just as a city set on a hill cannot be hidden, no disciple of Jesus can remain unnoticed in the world. It would be absurd to think that a person would deliberately conceal his light. One does not place a lamp under a bowl but on an ele-

> vated stand where it can be seen. Similarly it would be absurd to think that a person from whom no light shines could belong to the light of the world.

Without drawing unnecessary attention to the literary technique of this cluster of images, Ridderbos articulates their distinctive contributions to Jesus' point about the disciples' influence upon the world.

(1) disciples : earth = salt : food
with respect to preservative effect (benefit of influence)

(2) disciples' good works : world = light : whatever it illuminates
with respect to inspiration and joy (means of influence)

(3) disciples' conspicuousness : world = city on a hill : those who see it
with respect to strong mental impression (irresistibility of influence)

(4) disciples' works : world = lamp : interior of a house
with respect to the futility of concealment (obligation for influence)

For another interpretive model see Lambrecht (85–109) on the "Parables in Mark 4."

EXERCISE

Exercise on the Wedding Guests, the Patched Garment, the Wineskins, and the Old and New Wine (Lk 5:33–39; cf. Mt 9:14–17; Mk 2:18–22)

Construct one formula for each of the four analogies in this discursive sequence. Does each make a special contribution of its own? Compare the formulas on pp. 62, 76, 47.

NARRATIVE SEQUENCES

John Bunyan said that a simple analogy of his, drawn perhaps from the image of pilgrims in Hebrews 11:13–14, grew by degrees into the whole narrative of *Pilgrim's Progress*. When two or more comparisons depict related situations, characters, or events they verge on becoming a story-parable. Thus the Servant in Authority (Mt 24:45–51; Lk 12:41–48).

INTERPRETIVE MODEL

Kistemaker, 127

> Jesus is represented by the master of the household. He leaves with the promise of his return. In the absence of Jesus, his followers are given privileges and responsibilities. If the believer is faithful and wise in the discharge of his duties, Jesus will reward him abundantly upon his return. But if he is unfaithful and behaves irresponsibly, Jesus' return will be an unexpected event for him which results in complete separation from the people of God along with fitting punishment.

What looks as if it will be a unified story ("Who then is the faithful and wise servant?") turns out to be a pair of alternative hypothetical cases. Kistemaker's interpretation involves a separate analogy for each outcome.

(1) responsible servant : his master = faithful follower : Jesus

with respect to promise of abundant reward

(2) irresponsible servant : his master = unfaithful follower : Jesus

with respect to promise of punishment

Luke 12:47–48 extends the narrative cluster.

(3) informed offender: his master = enlightened rebel: Jesus
with respect to promise of severe punishment

(4) uninformed offender : his master = unenlightened
    rebel: Jesus
with respect to promise of light punishment

Luke's alternative situations edge closer to the coherence of a single story. Matthew's pair hypothesizes two outcomes for one servant; Luke's version begins to look like one story about two servants. Though the Wise Builder and the Foolish Builder (Mt 7:24–27) are formally separate narratives, we usually give them one title such as "The Two Builders" because we perceive them as unified. One children's version depicts the two men building on adjacent properties—the foolish man finishing first and watching the other's patient labor, the wise man observing his neighbor's disaster from the safety of the rock. The text creates no such links of time, setting, or interaction. By contrast, in the Two Sons (Mt 21:28–32) the sons' actions are linked by their common association with their father; without such links, we would have two alternative images like those of the two builders, which we could properly distinguish as "The Disobedient Son" and "The Obedient Son." For practice, one might construct formulas to express the distinct but complementary points in both the Two Builders and the Two Sons. The Lost Son (Lk 15:11–32) links similar images on a larger scale; but here, as in the Two Sons, we have moved to *extended analogies*—described in part 1.5. Before we turn to that topic, we must note the presence of discrete symbols in some parables.

SYMBOLS IN PROPORTIONAL ANALOGIES

Another kind of cluster turns up in the parables when one feature of the image is a symbol in its own right. In John 10:11 Jesus said, "I am the good shepherd." Such a symbol implies a comparison just as a metaphor does, but sometimes a simpler one. Jesus' declaration describes relationships in a proportional analogy:

(1) Jesus : [disciples] = shepherd : [sheep]
with respect to sacrificial care

The first sentence, however, "I am the good shepherd," makes a distinct point about just one entity of the tenor.

(2) Jesus = shepherd
with respect to goodness

Here one image yields two kinds of analogies simultaneously: (1) is an equation of relationships; (2) is an equation of single entities. The proportion plainly implies a second symbol.

(3) the disciples = sheep
with respect to need for sacrificial care

We should ask of every analogy: Is there any pertinent equation of entities (in addition to the equation of relationships) that creates a symbol with a meaning of its own? There are some in the Lost Son (Lk 15:11–32).

INTERPRETIVE MODEL

Stein, 123

> Jesus ... seeks to defend before the Pharisees and scribes God's gracious offer of salvation to prodigals and the wrongness of their opposition to his ministry. ...
>
> While it is true that the main emphasis of Jesus in this parable is aimed not at describing the loving character of God, the fact remains that ... the character of God, described by the actions of the father in the parable, is integral to Jesus' main point. It is precisely this kind of God that Jesus' critics cannot envision. To use

> this parable therefore to describe the character of God
> is not to err in pressing details!

To gain his main aim in the parable Jesus must achieve a second goal. The main aim is to rebuke the Pharisees and scribes by showing that their relationship with God is no better than the elder son's relationship with his father.

> (1) the Pharisees and scribes : God = the elder son : the
> father
> with respect to misunderstanding of gracious forgiveness

But God must be like the gracious father, if the parable is to show that the Pharisees and scribes' unforgiving spirit is unlike God's. Hence Jesus' secondary purpose is to picture God's grace in the father's loving acts. Stein is too wary of allegorizing (56–61), but he rightly notes that Jesus equates the gracious father with God.

> (2) God = the father
> with respect to gracious forgiveness

Further, as Stein says, the Pharisees and scribes are wrong to oppose God's forgiveness. Thus Jesus' rebuke also includes a third goal: picturing the Pharisees and scribes' opposition in the elder brother's protest.

> (3) the Pharisees and scribes = the elder son
> with respect to wrongheaded response

Likewise Jesus equates the younger son with the despised tax collectors and "sinners" who, by coming to hear Jesus (Lk 15:1), intimate their change of heart.

> (4) tax collectors and sinners = the younger son
> with respect to past waywardness and present repentance

For additional interpretive models see Jeremias (119–20) on the Budding Fig Tree (Mk 13:28–29) and Lambrecht (48) on the Lost Son (Lk 15:11–32).

As we have seen in the Introduction, Jülicher and many others hold that each parable makes only one point, mistakenly supposing that the only alternative would be the allegorizing method that made separate points of every detail. Obviously there is more than one point in the Lost Son, but how do we determine where to draw the line so as not to allegorize the far country, its famine, citizens, swine, pods, the father's servants, robe, ring, shoes, and fatted calf? We need not worry now about oversymbolizing this parable while we ask the questions about its analogies that occupy us here in part 1. After we have considered what the topics of parts 2 and 3 can tell us about these questions, we will address them more fully in the conclusion ("Delimiting Allegory").

EXERCISE

Exercise on Matthew 7

This last part of the Sermon on the Mount is a series of analogies that are linked in various ways. Identify the separate analogies and construct the formulas necessary to express the points of these analogies. In expository form, indicate how the analogies work together to convey Jesus' message. Compare the formula on pp. 49, 109.

5

EXTENDED ANALOGIES

As we have seen, when Jesus is conveying a complex idea, he sometimes uses a *discursive sequence*—a series of analogies with vehicles that are not related by the subjects of their images, but only by their relevance to his argument. But often Jesus conveys a complex idea by elaborating a single image into a cluster of images that depict a single, unified situation or story. How are these analogies extended into allegory?

One way is by adding points of resemblance. Thus far we have usually found only one point of resemblance for each proportional equation—one respect in which the tenor and vehicle are related—though in the Sower (part 1.1) we noted four points of resemblance suggested by four different interpreters. Rather than disagreeing about which of them is correct, we should acknowledge that the image is allegorical because it makes these four points, and more besides. Another way is by adding equations, as we have seen in the Lost Son. Some parables, including the Lost Son, elaborate analogy into parable by both of these means.

TWO OR MORE POINTS OF RESEMBLANCE

Even brief comparisons often involve this kind of elaboration—as Boswell records in a conversation about religious toleration (539–40).

JOHNSON. "Sir, if a man is in doubt whether it would be better for him to expose himself to martyrdom or not, he should not do it. He must be convinced that he has a delegation [i.e., mandate] from heaven." GOLDSMITH. "I would consider whether there is the greater chance of good or evil upon the whole. If I see a man who had fallen into a well, I would wish to help him out; but if there is a greater probability that he shall pull me in, than that I shall pull him out, I would not attempt it. So were I to go to Turkey, I might wish to convert the Grand Signor to the Christian faith; but when I considered that I should probably be put to death without effectuating my purpose in any degree, I should keep myself quiet."

Goldsmith makes one analogy with numerous points of resemblance.

> Goldsmith : Grand Signor = Goldsmith : a man in a well
> with respect to: (1) awareness of need
>   (2) desire to help
>   (3) unlikelihood of helpfulness
>   (4) unwillingness to make the attempt

Likewise Jesus often chooses an image because it resembles his theme in more ways than one. The prodigal son resembles the tax collectors and sinners both in past waywardness and in present repentance. But interpreters who believe that "parables . . . have only one point of comparison" (Linnemann, 23) find Jesus' whole meaning in one similarity, and try to defend it against other exegetes' reasonable arguments for other similarities. Hence the competing titles for a single parable (e.g., Mk 4:26–29): the Seed Growing by Itself (Lambrecht, 99), the Seed Growing Secretly (Kistemaker, 30), the Patient Husbandman (Jeremias, 151).

Interpreters' rhetoric may conceal—from themselves and their readers—that their one point of resemblance actually includes two or more quite distinct features, as in Jeremias's comments on the Growing Seed (Mk 4:26–29).

INTERPRETIVE MODEL

Jeremias, 151–52

Once more the advent of the Kingdom of God is compared to the harvest. Again we are confronted with a sharp contrast; the inactivity of the farmer after sowing is vividly depicted: his life follows its ordered round of sleeping and waking, night and day; without his taking anxious thought ... or any active steps ... the seed grows from stalk to ear, and from ear to ripened corn—the naming of each stage of the process describes the unceasing process of growth. Then, suddenly, the moment arrives which rewards the patient waiting. The corn is ripe, the sickle is thrust in, the joyful cry rings out, "the harvest has come." ... Thus it is with the Kingdom of God; thus with the same certainty as the harvest comes for the husbandman after his long waiting, does God when his hour has come, when the eschatological term is complete, bring in the Last Judgment and the Kingdom. Man can do nothing with regard to it; he can only wait with the patience of the husbandman. ... It is a contrast-parable by which Jesus replied to the doubts about his mission, and to frustrated hopes. Consider the husbandman, says Jesus, who patiently awaits the time of the harvest. So, too, God's hour comes irresistibly. ... Till then it behoves man to wait in patience and not to try and anticipate God, but in full confidence to leave everything to him.

This is not one of Jeremias's four "double-edged" parables (131), and therefore he assumes that it makes only one point. But the acuteness of his common-sense practical criticism prevails over this constricting theory, for he has articulated no less than eight points of resemblance.

> humanity : advent of the kingdom = the farmer : the harvest
>
> with respect to (1) human unconcern,
> (2) inactivity,
> (3) patience,
> (4) and confidence;
> as well as the (5) length of the process
> and its (6) certainty,
> (7) unremitting activity,
> (8) and sudden conclusion

The first two points are explicit in Mark's text. "He does not know how" expresses (1); "all by itself" conveys (2). The rest Jeremias infers. "First the stalk, then the head, then the full kernel in the head" provides reasonably good warrant for (5) and (7); so does "As soon as the grain is ripe, he puts the sickle to it" for (8). But there is no warrant for asserting (3), though Jeremias's preferred title, "The Patient Husbandman," makes it the main point. Nor does the image entail certainty of harvest or the farmer's confidence. (The parable of the Sower details how easily a crop can fail.)

This overreading may be due to preconceptions about the kingdom, brought to the parable from Jeremias's theology about other biblical passages (160): "The contrast-parables express the confidence of Jesus in the face of doubt concerning his mission." Preconceptions are unavoidable, but we must test them in the light of the text. Jeremias's theology of the kingdom seems like the best explanation for his neglect of a ninth point of resemblance—the detail that makes some interpreters call it the Seed Growing Spontaneously (Mk 4:28, "All by itself the soil produces grain"). Not every detail must be symbolic, but one should show cause for ignoring anything so prominent.

Whenever the image of a parable elaborates events enough to deserve the term "story," it probably has at least two pertinent points of resemblance—differentiated as "before and after" or "earlier and later" (as in the Wedding Guests, Mk 2:18–20).

INTERPRETIVE MODEL

Hunter, 49–50

> Pious men, noting the grave faces of the Baptist's disciples and of the Pharisees, thought that fasting would have better befitted Jesus and his men. "Can the wedding guests (or 'the groomsmen') fast while the bridegroom is with them?" Jesus replied, making a veiled claim to Messiahship. "My disciples are as light-hearted as a wedding party. And why not? Kingdom time is no time for mourning."

Hunter's point in 2:19 concerns the disciples' *present*.

> disciples : Jesus = wedding guests : bridegroom
> with respect to their joy in his presence

But 2:20 makes a point of resemblance about the *future*. The real thrust of Mark's text depends on the contrast between the points about the present and the future, as Drury observes (44–45).

> disciples : Jesus = wedding guests : bridegroom
> with respect to their grief in his absence

Drury's references to 2 Corinthians and the Revelation identify an independent symbol as well: Jesus = bridegroom.

Here is conclusive evidence against Julicher's one-point theory; the message of this parable depends on the allegorical extension of the anology to include two points of resemblance between tenor and vehichle. See also Buttrick's exposition of the Sower (Mt 13:3–8).

Exercise on the Hidden Treasure (Mt 13:44)

Assume that this formula represents the essential equation.

kingdom partaker: kingdom = man : treasure

Note all the points of resemblance that you can perceive: one list of explicit points, one of points implied. Decide which belong to the reading you think is most appropriate, and write "with-respect-to" lines for them. Compare your results with the formula on p. 125. Try to detect all of the factors that influence your choices, including your theological preconceptions.

TWO OR MORE PROPORTIONAL EQUATIONS

On one memorable occasion when Jesus made a point by an analogy, his hearer took the liberty of pushing it to a second equation with a contrasting point—which Jesus accepted as appropriate (the Children's Bread, Mk 7:24–30; cf. Mt 15:21–28).

A woman whose little daughter was possessed by an evil spirit came and fell at his feet. The woman was a Greek, born in Syrian Phoenicia. She begged Jesus to drive the demon out of her daughter. "First let the children eat all they want," he told her, "for it is not right to take the children's bread and toss it to their dogs." "Yes, Lord," she replied, "but even the dogs under the table eat the children's crumbs." Then he told her, "For such a reply, you may go; the demon has left your daughter." She went home and found her child lying on the bed, and the demon gone.

In a blunt-sounding test of the woman's faith, Jesus makes one comparison.

> Greeks : Jews = dogs: children
> with respect to priority in care

But the woman responds to the challenge with grace born of faith, humility, and wit.

> God's mercy to Jews : Greeks = surplus of children's food : dogs
> with respect to sufficiency for both parties

In spontaneous talk a simple analogy often invites expansion. So it happens when Shakespeare's Portia is compelled by her dead father's will to marry only the man who makes the right choice from among three caskets of gold, silver, and lead. In *The Merchant of Venice*, 3.2.40–45, she is afraid that Bassanio will fail.

> Away then! I am lock'd in one of them;
> If you do love me, you will find me out.
> Nerissa and the rest, stand all aloof.
> Let music sound while he doth make his choice;
> Then if he lose he makes a swan-like end,
> Fading in music.

Her analogy reflects the folklore that dying swans sing:

> (1) Bassanio : the end of his courting = swan : its death
> with respect to musical accompaniment

To make her feelings more clear she brings herself into the "comparison" (45–47)—the word *proper* having its French sense, "(my) own":

> That the comparison
> May stand more proper, my eye shall be the stream
> And wat'ry death-bed for him.

As befits her agitation, this image makes a confused picture; and the point of resemblance may be elusive. But the basic logic is clear:

(2) Bassanio : Portia's tears = swan : the stream where it dies

with respect to ...

Even for such a simple image as this, the "one-point theory" is obviously inadequate. Portia has just one main idea in mind: "If Bassanio chooses the wrong casket I will be very sorry for both of us." But she has made two points in two analogies. A celebrated example of extended analogy is the conclusion of John Donne's "Valediction: Forbidding Mourning." The poet compares the unity-in-duality of his marriage with the two legs of a geometric compass; then he makes an elaborate, point-by-point comparison—between its operations in drawing a circle, and the feelings that go with his journeying away from his wife—all to assure her of a single point: that his absence will not damage their love.

Thus we can admit that Jesus made two or more points in a given parable and still affirm that he had one main point in mind. How can we identify it in the Two Debtors (Lk 7:41–47)?

INTERPRETIVE MODEL

Blomberg, 185–86

Not only do the three characters of the parable in some sense correspond to the three key individuals at dinner in Simon's house, but more specific lessons may easily be derived from each. *(1) Like the man owing fifty denarii, those who take their spiritual condition for granted and are not aware of having been forgiven of numerous gross wickednesses should not despise those who have been redeemed from a more pathetic state. (2) Like the debtor owing five hundred denarii, those who recognize they have much for which to be thankful will naturally respond in generous expressions of love for Jesus. (3) Like the creditor,*

God forgives both categories of sinners and allows them to begin again with a clean slate.

These three points are virtually spelled out, in turn, by verses 44–46 (contrasting the behavior of Simon and the woman) and verses 47–50 (the declaration of forgiveness). The second point undoubtedly forms the heart of Jesus' message on this occasion, but it may not be entirely divorced from the other two. . . .

To try to summarize the parable with one bland phrase, such as "salvation is only for sinners," misses crucial nuances that the narrative articulates.

Blomberg's excellent model first shows that the three principals have symbolic value.

(1) Simon the Pharisee = the debtor who is forgiven less
with respect to (a) small sense of sin
                        (b) small sense of gratitude

(2) woman anointing Jesus = the debtor who is forgiven more
with respect to (a) great sense of sin
                        (b) great sense of gratitude

(3) God = creditor
with respect to willingness to forgive all sinners who seek mercy

Second, it identifies three proportional analogies expressed in the text by the characters' relationships in pairs.

(1) Simon : woman = the debtor forgiven less : the debtor forgiven more
with respect to obligation not to be contemptuous

(2) woman : God = the debtor forgiven more : the creditor

with respect to response in generous expressions of love for
Jesus

(3) God : Simon and the woman = the creditor : both
debtors
with respect to willingness to forgive

Third, Blomberg attributes this allegory to Jesus himself, not to
secondary activity. He disposes of scholarly arguments that regard
Luke's story of Jesus, Simon, and the woman as a secondary addition artificially allegorizing what was at first a one-point parable.
He also shows that by itself Jesus' story reads like an allegory, and
that one-point interpretations simply fail to do the text justice.

How does the text justify Blomberg's judgment that the point
about the woman is "undoubtedly the heart of Jesus' message"?
One cue in *Luke's story* is the conflict's origin: what upsets Simon is
Jesus' calm reception of the woman's demonstrative, emotional out-
pouring. He cannot countenance it, or understand it as love. A cue
in *Jesus' story* is the order of the two debtors' appearances: the forgiveness of the great debt gets the climactic position at the story's
end. A *rhetorical* cue is the focus of Jesus' question which Blomberg
compares with Nathan's use of a parable to evoke David's judgment
upon himself. The Pharisee must admit that the woman loves Jesus
more than he does.

Likewise Jeremias (210–13), though in theory finding only
one point in the Unmerciful Servant (Mt 18:23–35), actually
describes nine significant points. As a general principle he
attributes allegorical features to the church's activity in transmit-
ting Jesus' words (66). Yet he responds to the manifest allegorical
correspondences in this story: "Behind the king we see God,
behind the debtor, the man who was allowed to hear the message
of forgiveness" (210).

God = king
first debtor = sinner offered forgiveness

His commentary clearly assumes a third correspondence:

second debtor = offender against sinner

His summary paragraph (213) distinguishes two points—an "exhortation" and a "warning." And he notes seven other points, stating some directly and leaving others implied in the connections between his comments and the three symbols above.

(1) God offers forgiveness (summary).

God : sinners = king : debtors
with respect to canceled obligation

(2) The penalty of our sin is beyond our capacity to pay ("the promise of v. 26 is impossible of fulfilment" [212]).

the sinner : sin = first debtor : huge debt
with respect to impossibility of propitiation

(3) Therefore God's mercy of forgiveness is "a merciful gift beyond conceiving" (summary; cf. "The king's mercy far exceeds the plea of his servant" [211]).

God : sin = king : huge debt
with respect to magnitude of undeserved mercy

(4) Others may be capable of restitution for their sins against us ("the promise . . . in v. 29 can be fulfilled" [212]).

other offenders : their sin against us = second debtor : small debt
with respect to possibility of restitution

(5) Nevertheless God expects us to forgive them freely (summary).

sinners : other offenders = first debtor : second debtor
with respect to obligation of forgiveness

(6) If we do not forgive them, God will refuse to forgive us (summary).

God : sinners = king : first debtor
with respect to punishment for failure to forgive

(7) God's punishment is frightful and endless ("frightfulness of the punishment ... [which] would be endless" [213]).

unforgiving sinners : punishment = first debtor : torture
with respect to endlessness of suffering

This legitimate kind of interpretation has frequently been confused with the allegorizing tradition that prevailed from the Fathers to the nineteenth century. Yet the differences are conclusive. The old allegorizers made symbols of every detail; Jeremias does not. Traditional allegorizers gave details of the parables arbitrary meanings that they brought to the text; all of Jeremias's symbolic associations have clear warrant in the text. He is not allegorizing (imposing symbols on the text); he is just recognizing the allegorical symbols in the text. Like Blomberg, Jeremias identifies the main points—in this case, the "exhortation" and the "warning." These choices are amply justified by Peter's question, and especially by Jesus' first reply (18:21–22): "Then Peter came to Jesus and asked, 'Lord, how many times shall I forgive my brother when he sins against me? Up to seven times?' Jesus answered, 'I tell you, not seven times, but seventy-seven times.'"

EXERCISE

Exercise on the Two Sons (Mt 21:28–32)

To interpret this parable follow the example of Jeremias and Blomberg. As far as the text warrants, identify symbols, formulate proportional equations, and determine point(s) of resemblance. Pay attention to the story's context (Mt 21:23–27), and give reasons for your choice of Jesus' main point(s). Compare the formulas on p.

104. For further practice do the same with the Great Supper (Lk 14:15–24) and the context of Luke 14:1–14, ignoring the parallel in Matthew 22:1–14 (its divergences unnecessarily complicate the exercise) and looking for a more complex theme than in the Two Sons with more symbols, proportional equations, and points of resemblance (compare the formulas on p. 8).

Even a three-word proverb, in context, can create an analogy of more than one proportional equation, as shown in Arndt's paraphrase (137–38) of Jesus' message, "Physician, heal yourself . . ." (Lk 4:23ff.).

(1) "You cannot believe My assertions outright."

Nazarenes : Jesus = prospective patients : unproven
  physician
with respect to skepticism

(2) "You demand that I do miracles."

Nazarenes : miracles at Nazareth = prospective patients :
  self-cure
with respect to demand for proof of competence

3) "You point to the report that in Capernaum I performed miraculous deeds, and now you insist that I should perform some among you, too; then you will believe."

miracles at Nazareth : miracles at Capernaum = self-cure :
  reported cures
with respect to disparate efficacy as proof

"Signs were demanded," Arndt says, "and such a demand always proceeds from skepticism and doubt." This implies that the third analogy carries Jesus' main point: "You must see for yourselves because you don't truly believe" (we might well call this parable the Skeptical Patients). One equation conveys most of Jesus' message, but the message depends on all three points. Those who cannot see in this saying "the slightest hint of a comparison" (Scharlemann, 16) are overlooking its immediate context. If we think of a parable first as an analogy, and only subsidiarily as a story, we will not focus exclusively on an image such as this, but look about for the tenor that it conveys.

EXERCISE

Exercise on the Physician for the Sick (Mk 2:16–17; Mt 9:11–12; Lk 5:30–32)

Study the context of this parable to draw out of Jesus' brief remarks the multiple correspondences of his analogy: symbols, proportional relationships, points of resemblance. What is his main point? Explain your conclusion. Compare the formula on p. 31.

The parable texts examined thus far provide interpretive cues in context and commentary, but not in a systematic list of symbolic correspondences. The parable of the Weeds (Mt 13:24–30, 36–43), however, gives us that kind of head start, though not all the symbolic consequences are made explicit.

INTERPRETIVE MODEL

Blomberg, 197–200

If the brief conclusions of other parables with only limited allegorical interpretations are generally regarded as inauthentic, then it is scarcely surprising that virtually all but the most conservative commentators vigorously deny that Jesus could have intended this parable to teach anything remotely resembling the specifics of Matthew 13:36–43.

A closer look, however, reveals some important structural similarities with the other triadic, monarchic parables. There is a central authority figure—the man who sows the seeds and oversees their harvest. There are contrasting subordinates—the wheat and the weeds. Nor is the symbolism of the interpretation ascribed to Jesus at all inappropriate. The use of seeds and plant growth to refer to righteous behavior had ample Old Testament precedent (cf., e.g., Hos 10:12; Jer 4:3–4; Is 55:10). The harvest was a standard metaphor for judgment. Unusual details suggest that the parable is meant to point to a second level of meaning. The enemy's coming stealthily to sow the tares and the farmer's refusal to make any attempt at weeding can both be explained by ancient horticultural practices but nevertheless remain atypical.

Even if the parable were left uninterpreted, it would seem fair to summarize its meaning under three headings, related to each of the main "characters." *(1) God permits the righteous and the wicked to coexist in the world, sometimes superficially indistinguishable from one another until the end of the age. (2) The wicked will eventually be separated out, judged and destroyed. (3) The righteous will be gathered together, rewarded and brought into God's presence. . . .*

Once the referents of the three main characters are identified, the other equations all fall into place naturally. God's enemy is obviously the devil. God's Word is preached throughout the world. The harvesters are the angels, who regularly figure in Jewish descriptions of the final judgment as God's helpers. The kingdom in verse 41, in keeping with Jesus' consistent use of the expression elsewhere in the Gospels, must refer to God's universal, sovereign reign rather than being equated with the church. Thus, the "contradiction" with verse 38 disappears.

Blomberg shows that the presence of allegory is no good reason to deny either the parable or the interpretation to Jesus. He notes seven explicit symbolic correspondences (13:37–39), and two others clearly implied (13:42–43; cf. 30).

Explicit

the Son of Man	=	man sowing seed
the field	=	world
sons of the kingdom	=	good seed
sons of the evil one	=	weeds
the devil	=	the enemy
the end of the age	=	harvest
angels	=	the harvesters

Implicit

evildoers thrown into the fiery furnace	=	burning weeds
kingdom of the Father	=	barn

His three-point summary of the meaning involves several points of resemblance.

(1) the righteous : the wicked = the wheat : the weeds with respect to coexistence by God's permission, to superficial indistinguishability and to persistence to the end of the age

(2) God : the wicked = the man sowing seed : the weeds with respect to separation, judgment, and destruction

(3) God : the righteous = the man sowing seed : the wheat with respect to gathering together, rewarding, and bringing into God's presence

One aspect of point 1, "God permits the righteous and the wicked to coexist in the world," involves yet another equation:

God's permission for coexistence = the man's decision to
  let the weeds grow

As Blomberg says, the symbols are not all equal in significance. His
summary makes no specific mention of the Son of Man, the field,
the devil, the angels, the fiery furnace, or the barn. Yet he acknowledges their supportive functions as details of the theme, and he distinguishes them from a feature with no symbolism—the servants.
Besides these non-symbolic persons there are non-symbolic
actions—sowing weeds, discovering them, and proposing to pull
them up—to be contrasted with the symbolic actions: the harvest,
the burning, the man's leaving the weeds to grow.

In this text interpreters find both more cues and fewer than
in other cases. Whereas the Two Debtors (Lk 7:41–47) only
implied the one-to-one correspondences of vehicle and tenor,
Luke's story provides a context for that parable that makes the
occasion obvious. Conversely, the parable of the Weeds spells out
the correspondences, but Matthew's story does not say why Jesus
tells this parable now. Thus far our models of interpretation have
focused mainly on determining the *meaning* of each parable, but
in this case the *application* needs special attention. The themes of
coexistence, judgment, and salvation are plain, but Blomberg must
answer two questions: to whom was the parable primarily
addressed, and why? In another part of his discussion (200) he
gives reasons for thinking that the disciples—the audience in
Matthew's story—are more likely to have been the original audience than the Pharisees and other separatists, as some scholars suggest. And he cites facts from the Gospels to show that the disciples needed encouragement to be patient and courageous. In the
process he also implies that the first of the three points in his summary is Jesus' "main point": the wicked and righteous must live
together in the world until the end of the age.

EXERCISE

Exercise on the Sower (Mk 4:3–8, 14–20)

Write an exposition covering not only the meaning of this parable as evident from the analogies themselves, but also Jesus' application of the parable to his audience, as that can be gathered from Mark's narrative. Use proportional formulas in your preliminary work, and justify your interpretive choices. Study the context carefully, especially Mark 4:1–2, 10–13, 33–34. Compare the formulas on pp. 33–34.

More useful interpretive models are Fay (65–81) on the parables of Mark 4, and Resseguie (288) on the Two Debtors (Lk 7:36–50).

6

DOUBLETS AND LARGER COMBINATIONS

Whereas analogy clusters add image to image to make successive points in a discourse (e.g., the Salt of the Earth, the Light of the World, etc., in Mt 5:13–16), parable *doublets* and larger combinations strengthen and explore a theme using two or more images for the same basic point. When two parables make exactly the same point, we may call their themes *congruent*. When two parables make overlapping but partly distinctive points, we may call their themes *complementary*.

CONGRUENT THEMES

One might find exactly the same meaning in the Wineskins as in the Patched Garment (Mk 2:21–22; Mt 9:16–17; Lk 5:36–38), and call their themes congruent.

(1) the old spiritual order : the kingdom = old garment : new cloth
with respect to incompatibility

(2) the old spiritual order : the kingdom = old wineskins : new wine
with respect to incompatibility

If so, Jesus' purpose in using repetition is for emphasis. But for the interpreter the repetition has the incidental but significant additional benefit of making it easier to determine exactly what is Jesus' main point. Standing alone without the Wineskins, the Patched Garment is ambiguous indeed, for it has several prominent features. Which is the crucial one that symbolizes Jesus' main point? The damage done to the garment? That is the occasion for the *action* of the parable. Is it the continuing worth of the old garment? That is the only apparent *motive* for patching at all. Is the crucial feature an implied alternative action, perhaps preparing the patch by soaking and shrinking it first? That is a possible solution to the *problem* of the situation. Or is it the fresh damage of the worse tear? That is the *outcome* of the action.

If we ignore the Wineskins, we have very little to help us determine Jesus' main point. But because we are dealing with a doublet, and because none of these features has any close correspondence in the Wineskins, we naturally look elsewhere for the point—to the most important feature of the Patched Garment that it shares with the Wineskins, the incompatibility of the old with the new. If Jesus has told both parables to make one point, we must find it not in their divergences, but in this common element. As two intersecting lines locate a point, so the two separate lines of thought in these two parables converge upon Jesus' point. We may then infer from the people's question (Mk 2:18) that the "old" and the "new" of Jesus' tenor must be the old spiritual order and the new kingdom.

Any doublet or larger combination among Jesus' parables may have this potential for guiding the interpreter to the main point. See also Blomberg (284–87) on the Mustard Seed and the Leaven (Mt 13:31–33; Mk 4:30–32; Lk 13:18–21).

COMPLEMENTARY THEMES

Some doublets and larger combinations overlap to reinforce a single idea, as above, and yet diverge enough for each image to supply its own implications. So it is in the hymn "Thy Word is Like a Garden, Lord," which uses successive comparisons of the Word of God with a garden, a mine, and an armory. Consider also Ecclesiastes 4:9–12; Isaiah 10:14–19; and Amos 5:18–19, or Shakespeare's Sonnet 73, which by turns compares approaching death with the end of an autumn, a day, and a fire. It may be difficult for a speaker or writer to find one analogy that covers all the features of a complex point. Alternatively, two or more overlapping analogies may serve the purpose—each supplying by its distinctive details what another lacks. Thus the Tower Builder and the Warring King (Lk 14:26–33).

INTERPRETIVE MODEL

Hunter, 65

> Jesus will have no rash disciples. Solemnly he warns all such to heed well the consequences. This is the *caveat* contained in the two parables of The Tower Builder and The Warring King, which probably come from the height of the Galilean Ministry when many were offering to follow him (Luke 9:57–62). . . .
>
> In the first parable Jesus says, "Sit down and reckon whether you can afford to follow me." In the second he says: "Sit down and reckon whether you can afford to refuse my demands."

On one hand, the two vehicles convey one common idea, identical in both parables.

(1) follower : prospective discipleship = builder : building of tower

with respect to preparedness for the consequences

(2) follower : prospective discipleship = king : encounter in war

with respect to preparedness for the consequences

On the other hand, Hunter sees in the differences that each image has its own point.

(3) follower : prospective discipleship = builder : building of tower
with respect to foreseeing the cost of the enterprise

(4) follower : demands of Jesus = king : demands of a stronger king
with respect to foreseeing the results of defiance

Apparently these two images reinforce a point *and* address its diverse implications. But which ones? Though Blomberg agrees with Hunter on the main point ("Would-be disciples must consider the commitment required to follow Christ"), he emphasizes a different distinction—"degree of seriousness."

INTERPRETIVE MODEL

Blomberg, 281

> The man who is unable to finish building a tower risks only ridicule from his community and the possible loss of financial investment. The man who fails to realize that he is outnumbered in battle risks losing his kingdom, his soldiers and his life. This difference suggests that the passage is arranged in a climactic sequence and explains why Jesus' conclusion seems still more severe: "Whoever of you does not renounce all that he has cannot be my disciple" (v. 33).

The effect that Blomberg describes is rhetorical, not a new point of resemblance. Should we accept Hunter's emphasis, or Blomberg's, or both? Parts 2 and 3 will help us decide such questions.

For another interpretive model see the exposition of the Lost Coin (Lk 15:8–10) by Bowie et al. (268–69).

Exercise on the Hidden Treasure and the Pearl (Mt 13:44–46)

Reconsider your interpretation of the Hidden Treasure (p. 63) in light of its doublet, the Pearl. List the features common to both images, and those peculiar to each, including persons, things, actions, and events. Which ones support your determination of Jesus' meaning? Why? Identify the main point(s) of this doublet and justify your decision. Compare the formulas on p. 94.

Parables can work together in larger groups than doublets. The triplet of Luke 15 is part of a scattered series defending Jesus' ministry to outcasts and "sinners" against the Pharisees' criticisms. Together they invoke more facts and judgments than any one parable can convey—some in the Lost Sheep, a slightly different set in the Lost Coin, while the Lost Son focuses on the Pharisees, and the Great Supper (Lk 14:15–24) has its own special emphasis, with its own selection of points, as many exegetes have acknowledged (e.g., Hunter, 56–57).

God : professedly religious = householder : original guests
with respect to choice of those favored with an invitation

professedly religious : Jesus = original guests : servant
with respect to refusal of the invitation

God : sinners and Gentiles = householder : those from
    street and highway
with respect to new invitation

The Great Supper stresses the perverse response of the self-righteous to Jesus' message; other parables emphasize other features of Jesus' conflict with pharisaical attitudes. They include the Physician for the Sick (Mk 2:16–17; Mt 9:11–12; Lk 5:30–32), the Vineyard Laborers (Mt 20:1–16), the Two Sons (Mt 21:28–32), the Two Debtors (Lk 7:41–47), and the Pharisee and the Publican (Lk 18:9–14). (This last parable, as well as three other example-stories—the Good Samaritan [Lk 10:25–37], the Rich Fool [Lk 12:13–21], and the Rich Man and Lazarus [Lk 16:19–31]—represent a different kind of analogy from the bulk of Jesus' story-parables [Sider 1981].) Somewhere in this group of parables Jesus makes the following points; each parable makes at least several of them. I have not, for the sake of my argument, distinguished these points with unusual narrowness; most have been identified by interpreters as the sole main point of one parable or another.

1. The "sinners" have rebelled against God.
2. In consequence they are in great need.
3. They know they need spiritual help.
4. They are repentant.
5. They feel unworthy of God's grace.
6. But they seek after God anyway.
7. They accept his grace gladly.
8. Their gratitude and love for God are correspondingly great.
9. The Pharisees have tried hard to please God.
10. They are proud of their efforts.
11. They feel little or no need for repentance and forgiveness.
12. Their gratitude and love for God are correspondingly small.
13. They regard "sinners" as undeserving of God's favor.
14. They despise them and feel superior to them.
15. They resist the idea that God would show mercy to "sinners."
16. This sinful resistance separates them from God.
17. But they do not recognize their need for spiritual help.

18. God forgives repentant sinners.
19. His mercy to them is just.
20. It surpasses their expectations.
21. He rejoices in their salvation.
22. He expects the "righteous" to do likewise, acknowledging their own need.
23. He accepts them if they do so.
24. He resists the self-righteously superior.
25. They are, in fact, spiritually inferior to the repentant "sinners."
26. His judgment upon them surpasses their expectations.

In each parable Jesus uses several distinct *ideas* to produce a unified *effect*.

Interpreting a parable means, first of all, asking questions about how it works as an analogy. What point(s) does it make? Which should be regarded as the main point(s)? What equation(s)—positive, negative, or *a fortiori*—does the analogy state or imply? What point(s) of resemblance, stated and implied, are pertinent to each equation? What details—of image, of Jesus' discourse, or of context—appear not to suggest an equation or point of resemblance? But a parable also includes all the features discussed in parts 2 and 3. Therefore, according to what we learn from them, our tentative interpretations and trial formulas at this point must be augmented, modified, tested, and confirmed or rejected.

CHAPTER

7

DEFINING THE PARABLE

Thus far our purview of Jesus' "parables," strictly understood, has included both too much and too little.

On one hand, we acknowledge too little until we take account of Jesus' historical parables. Before turning to them we should note that on the other hand we have acknowledged too much within the scope of the parable, by including in our analysis some simple metaphors and similes. These must be distinguished from "parables" if we are to respect the evangelists' use of *parabolē*. They reserve the term for analogies more or less devoted to the service of *argumentation*. The more elaborate the image, the more prominent the function of rational argument usually becomes. Not so with typical simple comparisons—in simile or metaphor—such as calling a person a hawk or dove, or a snake in the grass. Usually these appeal mainly to the five senses, the emotions, and the imagination. When Jesus says of Herod: "Go tell that fox 'I will drive out demons'" (Lk 13:32), the effect is intuitive and so swift that one hardly thinks of the rational argument implied. The more elaborate kind of comparison may still have intuitive force, but only that kind presents itself as a rational argument. There are exceptions and ambiguous cases; we have seen that a phrase like "Physician, heal yourself" can be shorthand for an elaborate argument. But the functional distinction has justified scholars' longstanding practice of studying the parables without considering all of Jesus' similes and metaphors.

A FUNCTIONAL DEFINITION

Every *parabole* so labeled in the Gospels involves more than one point of resemblance, or more than one equation. The texts invite this functional definition for a parable: *a discursive or narrative analogy in the service of moral or spiritual argument.*

This definition ignores, but by no means denies, the parables' pervasive intuitive force (cf. part 2.9). Some interpreters play down this extrarational dimension (e.g., Jülicher, Linnemann, Kahlfeld); others tend to forget everything else (e.g., Crossan, Funk 1975, TeSelle, and Perrin 1976). Yet only purely technical terms can avoid connotation, and only a very peculiar kind of poetic language even tries to escape denotation. Confining Jesus' parables to either hemisphere of language may be an attempt to get more from his words, but the end result is always less. It is a contemporary commonplace that our intuitive grasp of such symbols' intimations may point the way to their true rational force, but the converse is equally true. What we make of the parables as argument can open up new possibilities for our intuitive response.

HISTORICAL PARABLES

This definition of *parable* covers analogies that Jesus drew from current events and Old Testament history. Though Beare (474) refers to "the parable of the Flood" and Jeremias uses similar language, the analogies in the following list are seldom considered with the parables, perhaps because none is so labeled in the Gospels, or perhaps because most of the sayings that the evangelists label as *parabolai* are apparently hypothetical or fictional rather than historical. Good exegetes, however, see the same kind of argumentation in them—e.g., Moorman (160–61) on current events in Luke 13:1–5, the Murdered Galileans and Victims of Siloam, and Ridderbos (229) on David and the Consecrated Bread (Mt 12:1–8; cf. Mk 2:23–28; Lk 6:1–5). And there are precedents in

Old Testament prophecy (e.g., Is 54:9–10, Ezek 14:12–14). Jesus'
analogies from history also include the following.

	Matthew	Luke	John
Elijah and Elisha		4:24–27	
Sodom, Tyre, and Sidon (cf. Ezek 28)	11:20–24	10:12–15	
Priests in the Temple	12:1–2, 5–6		
Jonah and Nineveh	12:39–41	11:29–30, 32	
Solomon and the Queen of the South	12:42	11:31	
Days of Noah	24:37–39	17:26–27	
Days of Lot			17:28–30
Lot's Wife			17:32–33
Moses and the Serpent			3:14–15

PARABLES IN JOHN

The functions of analogy are as pertinent to the fourth Gospel
as they are to the Synoptics, though studies of the parables have
neglected those in John. It is only partly true that in John "the use
of standing symbols for certain abstract ideas—light, water, bread,
and the like—belongs to a different way of thinking from the realistic observation of nature and human life which supplies the
material of the Synoptic parables" (Dodd 1963, 366). Jesus occasionally uses this "different way of thinking" in the Synoptics too
(e.g., Jeremias, 119–20, on the Budding Fig Tree). And though
Johannine metaphors introduced with Jesus' "I am" are missing in
Matthew, Mark, and Luke, in the Synoptics Jesus is sometimes the
parabolic subject by tacit symbolism—e.g., the Sower (Lambrecht,
103–4), the servant in the Great Supper (Hunter, 57), the son in
the Tenants (Jeremias, 72). Most analogies in John resemble at
least some synoptic parables in their essentials: content of the
images (e.g., harvest, growing seeds and plants, sheep, bride-

groom), analogic structure of the thought (e.g., the Good Shepherd), and even rhetorical structures.

It is a scholarly commonplace that if Jesus spoke as he is represented in the Synoptics, he cannot have spoken as he is represented in John. Yet the true rhetorical affinities of the parables in John with certain synoptic parables are highly significant. There are numerous examples in Dodd (1963, 386ff.) and two more in Drury (160–62). There is also a significant parallel between the Vine and Branches (Jn 15:5–8) and the Light of the World (Mt 5:14–16). Both analogies are discourses based in a literal description of the disciples' responsibilities, sprinkled with metaphors (in quotation marks below) that create a coherent pictorial image. Some statements (in parentheses) elaborate this image without any literal reference to the disciples at all. And the mundane image thus elaborated is linked with the spiritual tenor of Jesus' literal discourse by explicit terms of comparison (in italics).

Matthew 5:14–16	John 15:5–8
Basic Situation	
You are the "light" of the world.	I am the "vine"; you are the "branches."
Potential Positive Outcome	
(A city on a hill cannot be hidden.)	If a man remains "in" me and I "in" him, he will "bear" much "fruit";
Potential Negative Outcome	
(Neither do people light a lamp and put it under a bowl.)	apart from me you can do nothing. If anyone does not remain "in" me, he is *like* a branch (that is thrown away and withers; such branches are picked up, thrown into the fire and burned).

Potential Positive Outcome

(Instead they put it on its stand, and it gives light to everyone in the house.) *In the same way* let your "light shine" before men, that they may see your good deeds and praise your Father in heaven.

If you remain "in" me and my words remain in you, ask whatever you wish, and it will be given you. This is to my Father's glory, that you "bear" much "fruit," showing yourselves to be my disciples.

The divergences are obvious: the elements occur in somewhat differing sequences; the structure of sentences varies; John's initial equation is double and Matthew's single; Matthew's City on a Hill (an independent image functioning as doublet for the Lamp on a Stand) has no parallel in John's language; and John 15:5–8 is a reiteration (with alterations) of 15:1–4—a passage with no analogue in Matthew's language. Yet the similarities are enough to show that John's method here is not unique in the Gospels (cf. also Jn 3:14 with Mt 12:40, and Jn 2:18–20 with Lk 2:48–50).

When we have grasped the fact that Jesus' parables are analogies first and foremost, and when we have analyzed the basic workings of analogy extended into allegory, it becomes evident that the interpreter's chief responsibility and greatest challenge is to determine, as far as possible, which features of a parable are symbolic and which are not. But we will defer to the conclusion of this book the question of "Delimiting Allegory," because most of the available resources are yet to be explored. In part 2 we consider the cues to be found in the internal features of the parables, and in part 3, the cues to be found in external considerations. Because a feature that provides conclusive evidence for one parable may be useless for another, any full-dress interpretation of a parable should leave no stone unturned. Any one of the topics in parts 2 and 3 might prove to be the only certain cue to Jesus' precise meaning.

SUMMARY OF PART I

1. Almost all of Jesus' parables convey their meaning by *analogy* in one or more *proportional equations;* e.g., sinners : God = the lost son : his father (Lk 15:11–32). (The exceptions are four *example-stories.*)

2. The analogy in a parable compares the author's *tenor* on theme (e.g., sinners and God) with the author's chosen *vehicle* (e.g., the lost son and his father); the vehicle is a concrete and vivid *image*—sometimes simply *pictorial* (e.g., the Budding Fig Tree, Mk 13:28–29), but often elaborated with character(s) and action(s) into *narrative* (story).

3. A single feature of the image may be an *independent symbol* (e.g., God = the lost son's father).

4. The meaning of the comparison depends on some specific *point of resemblance* between the tenor and the vehicle; e.g., sinners : God = the lost son : his father, with respect to grievous offense.

5. The comparison of a parable may actually be a *contrast* ($\neq$); or it may be an equation of *unequals* ($<$) or ($>$).

6. Parables may occur in *pairs or clusters,* as Jesus moves from one topic of his message to another (e.g., the parables of Mk 4), or in *doublets* and *triplets,* as he employs more than one parable to emphasize or elaborate a single topic of his message (e.g., the Lost Sheep, Coin, and Son, Lk 15:1–32).

7. Parables may be *extended analogies.* They may create more than one point of resemblance; e.g., sinners : God = the lost son : his father, with respect to (1) grievous offense, (2) desire for mercy, etc. Or they may consist of more than one proportional equation; e.g., (1) sinners :

God = the lost son : his father; (2) Pharisees : God = the elder son : his father; (3) Pharisees : sinners = the elder son : the lost son.

8. The parable in Jesus' use is *a discursive or narrative analogy in the service of moral or spiritual argument.* This definition applies to sayings of Jesus not commonly acknowledged as parables: historical parables, e.g., Elijah and Elisha (Lk 4:24–27) and parabolic sayings in John, e.g., the Vine and Branches (15:5–8).

9. Extended analogies are *allegorical.* To determine the limits of allegorical symbolism in a parable, interpreters must study all its pertinent features—both internal (part 2) and external (part 3).

PART
II

Internal Features of the Parables

Any of the internal features of a parable—language, plot, characters, dialogue, setting, point of view, or tone— may interest the reader for its own sake; that is the nature of vivid image-making and storytelling. But the interpreter's main interest must focus on how these features can help us determine Jesus' main point, and how they can guide us in "drawing the line" between the details that have symbolic import and those that do not. We begin with the simplest elements, individual words and phrases.

CHAPTER

1

DICTION

A picture may be worth a thousand words, but Jesus could create one with just a few. Often the meaning of a parable comes down to one or two words. *Diction* is a term denoting an author's choice of particular words.

DENOTATION

In analyzing diction we are likely to focus first on the rational content of the words—their *denotation*. Jesus' exact words for the vehicle of the Leaven (Mt 13:33) may help us choose from among various renderings of the tenor.

INTERPRETIVE MODEL

Gundry, 269

> Oddly, the text reads that the woman "hid" the leaven in the flour, as though the large amount of flour engulfed the small amount of leaven (cf. the smallness of the mustard seed).

Why such an unusual word choice? The peculiarity of Jesus' language may invite us to rule out the *pervasiveness of effect* (so Kistemaker above, part 1.2).

kingdom : [the world] = yeast : dough

with respect to pervasiveness

The use of "hid" also may help the case for either the contrast of small beginnings with great results or the obscurity or hiddenness of the kingdom's beginnings.

(1) [beginnings of kingdom : culmination of kingdom] = mustard seed : "tree"

with respect to [contrast of size] (implied in "hid")

(2) [beginnings of kingdom : culmination of kingdom] = mustard seed : "tree"

with respect to obscurity (explicit in "hid")

Almost any nuance of a word may provide invaluable guidance for interpretive choices such as these.

EXERCISE

Exercise on the Pearl (Mt 13:45–46)

According to Stein (101), "we have a merchant seeking to buy pearls. The Greek term used to describe this 'merchant' is *emporos* and indicates that the man in this parable is not a shopkeeper but a wholesale trader or dealer who was involved in the purchasing of pearls." If this merchant is a trader in pearls rather than a collector, what does the denotation of *emporos* imply about his selling everything to possess this one pearl? If that is the key to Jesus' main point, which of these alternatives best expresses it?

the new believer : the kingdom = the merchant : the pearl
with respect to (1) joy of discovery
(2) singleness of purpose
(3) ability to pay one's way

For other good models of interpretation focused on denotation see Scott (121–22) and Talbert (147–48) on the Lost Son,

Stein (111–12) on the Unjust Steward, Linnemann (62–63) on the Pharisee and Publican, and Kilgallen (1993, 45–48) on the Empty House.

CONNOTATION

There is more to the meaning of a parable, however, than the logical argumentation of the analogy. It is therefore not enough to determine the rational denotation of Jesus' or the evangelists' words, whenever their audience also attached to them an emotional association or *connotation*. In the Lost Son (Lk 15:11–32), for example, "'Sinner' has a connotation that goes beyond our usual moralistic interpretation and involves a disreputable social status" (Talbert, 147–48). We have to add the Pharisees' social superiority to their moral disgust in order to appreciate the full force of their contempt for some of the company that Jesus received and of his rejoinders in the Lost Sheep, Coin, and Son. The socialization of Jesus' audience defines the connotations of words like "sinners" as well as "slave" (Beare, 477) in the Servant in Authority (Mt 24:45–51; Lk 12:41–48), and the repulsive language in the Barren Fig Tree (Lk 13:6–9).

INTERPRETIVE MODEL

Bailey, 1980, 84

The word "manure" (*koprion*) occurs only here in the New Testament. It is not the kind of language that is ordinarily used in religious illustrations. The vinedresser could have offered to spread on fresh earth, or water the tree each day, or even prune it back. If the fig tree represents the scribes and the chief priests, and the parable talks of the need to cast on some manure, then we have a clear case of what the comedians call "insult humor." . . . Mild irreverence for people in positions of power is usually appreciated by a popular audience. With such details the sparkle and vitality of the parable appears along with its unmistakable cutting edge.

Jesus' frequent ironies, noted in part 2.3, make Bailey's argument highly plausible. To grasp the force of the parables fully we must imagine the emotional effect of Jesus' language on his audience.

Connotation can affect other features, such as the characterizations and relationships found in the Lost Son (Lk 15:11–32).

INTERPRETIVE MODEL

Stein, 121

Throughout the parable titles of address have been used up to this point [15:27, 29]. The absence of a title of address by the older son to his father is therefore most noticeable. The older son, despite all his claim of loyalty to his father's commands (15:29), does not give his father the loving respect that he deserves. He is more concerned with his father's commandments than with his father! Surely Jesus in this portrayal had in mind those religious enthusiasts ... who kept the jot and tittle of what they thought was the law of God but whose hearts were nevertheless far from him. Finally we must note how the older brother refers to his younger brother—"this son of yours" (15:30). . . . The older brother simply will not acknowledge the prodigal as his brother. Again Jesus has brilliantly captured and portrayed the attitude of his opponents, the Pharisees and scribes, who would in no way accept their fellow Jews who were publicans and sinners as brothers.

Here Stein invokes the connotation of *polite forms of address*, and their absence, to characterize the elder son as disrespectful, and to show the tension in his relationship with his father. Stein also notes the evasive language that marks his aloof contempt for his brother. By revealing character these connotations contribute to the spiritual tenor, as expressed in the three formulas below. Thus, while noting the secondary significance of the father's relationship with the younger son (1), Stein locates the main point of the parable in the elder son's strained relationship with his father (2), and finds the distinctive significance of that relationship in the connotations of the elder son's language about his brother (3).

(1) God : tax collectors and sinners = father : younger son
with respect to gracious forgiveness

(2) Pharisees and scribes : God = elder son : the father
with respect to misunderstanding of gracious forgiveness

(3) Pharisees and scribes : tax collectors and sinners =
    elder son : younger son
with respect to aloof contempt

EXERCISE

Exercises on the Lost Son (Lk 15:11–32), the Vineyard Laborers (Mt 20:1–16), and the Good Samaritan (Lk 10:25–37)

1. For Luke 15:16b in the Lost Son, some ancient manuscripts read "He longed *to fill his belly with* the pods that the pigs were eating." Others read *to feed on*. What different messages do the two readings convey about how the prodigal is feeling? How are Jesus' hearers' *emotions* diversely affected? What difference, perhaps subtle, do the readings create in the *ideas* of the parable?

2. In the parable of the Vineyard Laborers, what does the omission of a polite address on the part of the all-day workers (Mt 20:12) tell us about their state of mind? What does the employer's polite address in response (20:13) tell us about his? How do these effects, in turn, contribute to the spiritual tenor

of the parable? For the sake of preciseness, formulate your conclusions in one or more proportional analogies.

3.   In the parable of the Good Samaritan, what does the lawyer's evasive phrase "The one who had mercy" (Lk 10:37) tell us about him? How does this effect help define Jesus' demands as conveyed by the parable, and what does it intimate about the lawyer's response?

SENSORY EFFECTS

Why do some words especially stimulate the imagination with impressions of sight, sound, touch, etc.? Why do some people respond more strongly than others to the same sensory language? The power of words to excite the senses is so personal and subjective that it seldom figures in lexical definitions. In order to grasp these nuances one must know Greek or Hebrew much better than what is necessary just to grasp denotation or even connotation of texts such as the Good Samaritan (Lk 10:25–37). Lacking such skills, one may turn to experts such as Bailey for a word's full impact.

INTERPRETIVE MODEL

Bailey, 1980, 48

> The Greek word "compassion" (*splanchnizomai*) has at its root the word "innards" (*splanchnon*). It is a very strong word in both Greek and Semitic imagery.... Indeed, the Samaritan has a deep "gut level reaction" to the wounded man. The Old Syriac version reflects the intensity of this word by translating, "He was compassionate to him and showed mercy," using two strong verbs. The Samaritan is not a gentile. He is bound by the same Torah that also tells him that his neighbor is his countryman and kinsman. He is traveling in *Judea*

and it is less likely for him than for the priest and the Levite that the anonymous wounded man is a neighbor. In spite of this, *he* is the one who acts.

Many sensory effects survive translation. For in the biblical languages, just as in English, concrete diction stimulates the sensory imagination more than abstract language can (e.g., *hug* vs. *love*); so does particular language more than general (e.g., *man* > *Jew* > *Pharisee* > *Nicodemus*). Thus the decking of the prodigal is not just social symbolism; the best robe, the ring, and the shoes make the younger son the most vivid visual feature of the story—for an obvious purpose. Compare the *auditory* effects of "music and dancing" (Lk 15:25).

EXERCISE

Exercise on the Strong Man Bound (Lk 11:19–22; cf. Mk 3:26–27), the Great Supper (Lk 14:15–24; cf. the Wedding Feast, Mt 22:1–14), and the Days of Noah and Lot (Lk 17:26–30; cf. Mt 24:37–39)

Luke's versions are richer by several details than Mark's picture or the scenes in Matthew (cf. Lk 11:21–22 with Mt 22:10), especially the extra scene, loaded with details, in Luke 17:28–29. What are the visual differences? How might these effects enhance the impact of Jesus' theme?

EXERCISE

Exercise on the Cup and Plate, and the Whitewashed Sepulchers (Mt 23:25–28)

Some of Jesus' most vivid language appears in brief comparisons like these. Articulate the sensory (and connotative) effects of (a) a cup or dish that looks clean until you look inside, and (b) the contrast between the inside and outside of a Palestinian tomb. How do these effects strengthen Jesus' point?

The Greek *grammatical structure* of sentences may be just as valuable a cue as diction. Since there is little to distinguish the significance of grammar in the parables from its significance elsewhere in the New Testament, one may apply to the parables the principles of analysis found in general textbooks on hermeneutics.

2

RHETORICAL STRUCTURES

Sometimes we are reminded that "what you say"—the denotation and connotation—may be no more important than "how you say it"—the effect of *rhetoric*. The devices of rhetoric are staggeringly numerous and varied (they include allegory), but *parallelism* and *repetition* are especially important structures of rhetoric in the parables.

REPETITION

Repeated words and phrases can be keys to a parable's meaning. In the Unmerciful Servant (Mt 18:23–35) Donahue (75–76) identifies a rhetorically pointed repetition—the plea to "have patience"—which highlights the similarity between the two situations. As a result, this parallel creates the *characterization* of the first servant in his exceeding "brutality," the *theme* of moral irony, and the *shift of our sympathies* away from the first servant. Not only are the similarities of situation significant, but also the ironic differences: the second demand for payment was practical and realistic; and, most important, the forgiveness of the first instance is not replicated in the second.

EXERCISE

Exercises on the Lost Son (Lk 15:11–32) and the Unjust Judge (Lk 18:1–8)

1. What does the father's repetition of his own words (24, 32) convey about his character, his relationships with each son,

and the resolution of the plot? Note any differences as well as similarities.

2.   A repeated phrase in the Unjust Judge creates the incongruity that we feel when for comic effect a common phrase (e.g., "From all over England young men flocked to join the few") is dislocated from its rhetorical context (e.g., "Please, sir, I want to join the few"). The conventional rhetoric of Luke 18:2 states that the judge "neither feared God nor regarded man." What is odd then about the repetition in the judge's mouth? What might it suggest about Jesus' characterization of the judge? Assume that the following formula expresses the parable's main point.

God : his chosen ones > the judge : the woman
with respect to promptness of vindication

What could the repetition imply for this point?

PARALLELISM

A pair of statements may be constructed in *step parallelism*, with their parts in consecutive correspondence, as in the Two Builders (Mt 7:24–27).

A Therefore everyone who hears these words of mine
    B and puts them into practice
        C is like a wise man
            D who built his house on the rock.
                E The rain came down, the streams rose, and the winds blew and beat against that house;
                F yet it did not fall,
because it had its foundation on the rock.

A But everyone who hears these words of mine
    B and does not put them into practice

C is like a foolish man
> D who built his house on sand.
>> E The rain came down, and the streams rose, and the winds blew and beat against that house,
>>> F and it fell

with a great crash.

Because pairs A and E are identical or as close as synonyms, we call the parallelism *synonymous*. Because pairs B, C, D, and F involve some element of contradiction (e.g., does/does not, fell/did not fall) or contrast (e.g., wise man/foolish man, rock/sand) we call their parallelism *antithetical*.

The conclusions break the parallelism, but they do not spoil it. For the rhythm of correspondences, strongly established by six parallel elements, creates (perhaps only subliminally) an expectation that the second sentence will end with "because it had its foundation on sand." Matthew's text exploits this expectation by an unexpected substitution (Gundry, 136). First, the "refusal to say that the second house was founded on sand . . . shows that sand hardly qualifies to be a foundation." Second: "Instead of giving a reason for the fall of the second house (as v 25 gives the reason why the first house did not fall), Matthew emphasizes the disaster. . . . The greatness of the fall consists in the completeness of the destruction. Thus the parable ends with a sober warning."

A series of parallel elements may also create a purposeful *anticlimax*, as in the Sower (Mk 4:3–8; Mt 13:3–9).

INTERPRETIVE MODEL

Gundry, 254

Though Mark's numbers—thirtyfold, sixtyfold, a hundredfold—build up to a climax, Matthew reverses their order so as to put "a hundredfold" first as the best example. The hundredfold contrasts with the less desirable yields of sixtyfold and thirtyfold, each introduced with an adversative δέ in place of Mark's καί. The adversative highlights the decrease in desirability.

Both in the Two Builders and in the Sower, the similarities set us up for the concluding contrast. This strategy depends on *significant difference* against a background of *general similarity*.

EXERCISE

Exercise on the Two Sons (Mt 21:28–32)

For this exercise we will ignore the textual variants in the parallelism (*The Greek New Testament,* ed. K. Aland et al., 3d ed. [New York: United Bible Societies, 1975]) and diverge slightly from the NIV reading. The first part has the following constituents.

A What do you think? There was a man who had two sons.
  B He went to the first
    C and said, "Son, go and work today in the vineyard."
      D He answered,
        E "I will not";
          F but later he changed his mind and went.

Set up verse 30 in lettered sections to show its correspondence, by step-parallelism, to verses 28–29. Which pairs of lettered sections are synonymous parallels? Which are antithetical parallels? Which of the lettered sections in verses 28–29 has no parallel in verse 30? Where can we find a parallel for this section in the verses following? Assuming that the following formula expresses the parable's main point, what does the repetition imply about it?

publicans and harlots : priests and elders = second son : first son
with respect to genuine obedience

A pair of statements (or larger structures) may also be constructed in *inverted parallelism*, so that the elements of the first correspond in reverse order with the elements of the second (e.g., the Two Masters, Mt 6:24).

> No one can serve two masters.
>   A Either he will hate the one
>   B and love the other,
>   B or he will be devoted to the one
>   A and despise the other.
> You cannot serve both God and Money.

This simplest form, ABBA, is called *chiasmus* because the form of the Greek character X (chi) diagrams the corresponding elements when the inverted pairs are set in parallel:

> either he will hate the one   and love the other
>   A   B
>   X
>   B   A
> or he will be devoted to the one   and despise the other

This may seem more like a trick of style than a real cue to meaning, but form does reinforce sense, for the tenor has the double prominence of first and last positions: "No one can serve two masters; . . . you cannot serve both God and Money."

The possibilities for parallel structures encompass larger units than single words and sentences, as in the Good Samaritan (Lk 10:25–37).

INTERPRETIVE MODEL

Bailey, 1980, 34

> Shortened to the main themes the full dialogue is as follows:

Round one: A lawyer stood up to put him to the test and said,

(1) Lawyer: (Question 1) "What must I *do* to inherit eternal *life?*"

    (2) Jesus: (Question 2) "What about the law?"

    (3) Lawyer: (Answer to 2) "Love God and your neighbor."

    (4) Jesus: (Answer to 1) "*Do* this and *live.*"

Round Two: He (the lawyer), desiring to *justify himself*, said,

(5) Lawyer: (Question 3) "Who is my neighbor?"

    (6) Jesus: (Question 4) "A certain man went down from Jerusalem . . ."

    "Which of these three became a neighbor?"

    (7) Lawyer: (Answer to 4) "The one who showed mercy on him."

(8) Jesus: (Answer to 3) "Go and continue *doing* likewise."

A number of important features tie the two dialogues together. (1) In each case there are two questions and two answers. (2) In each the lawyer asks the first question, but rather than answer his question Jesus poses a second. (3) In each round the lawyer then answers this second question. (4) Each round closes with Jesus' answer to the initial question. . . . (5) The first dialogue focuses on the question of *doing* something to inherit eternal life. On examination, so does the second. Desiring to "justify himself" he asks for a definition of his neighbor. Clearly he is still asking what he must do to gain eternal life. (6) Each round is introduced with an analysis of the motives of the lawyer. In the first we are told that he wants to test Jesus. In the second we find that he wants to justify himself. (7) Each round ends with instructions on what to *do*. Thus a long series of interlocking themes makes clear that the two rounds of dialogue are parallel halves of the same discussion.

The four pairs of questions and answers assume the sequence ABBA CDDC. Bailey's progression from formal analysis to interpretation is instructive. His first four points have to do with *form*—the doubly symmetrical ordering of speakers, of questions and answers. These formal considerations inspire questions about *content:* the lawyer's motives, and "doing" to gain eternal life. Rhetorical analysis should always ask: What does the form tell us about the meaning?

No rules for analysis can fully account for the semantic diversity of the language. For example, points of prominence—the beginning, middle, and end—sometimes locate the main point of Jesus' analogy, but not always. The necessary creativity of exegesis includes allowing each text to dictate its own interpretive questions. The more extensive and complex the rhetorical units, the more subjective the judgments we make in distinguishing their constituent parts. Thus Lambrecht offers one analysis of Mark 4 (86–88) and Donahue another (30–31). One might incline strongly toward either. We could devise others. Even without deciding which was in Jesus' mind or Mark's, we can learn from each one.

EXERCISE

Exercises on the Rich Man and Lazarus (Lk 16:19–31) and the Sheep and Goats (Mt 25:31–46)

1. The narrative prelude to the dialogue of the Rich Man and Lazarus displays an inverted parallelism of *basic situations,* each pair creating an antithesis.

    A (v 19) The rich man flourishes in wealth.

        B (vv 20–21) Lazarus, in misery, looks on.

> C (v 22a) Lazarus dies and is carried away by angels.
> C (v 22b) The rich man dies and is buried.
> B (v 23a) The rich man, in misery, looks on.
> A (v 23b) Lazarus flourishes in Abraham's bosom.

Arrange the text of verses 19–23, using alphabetical characters as labels, so as to show the extent of the inverted parallelism of *language*. As in Old Testament poetry the parallelisms are fashioned out of ideas (situation and character, here) as well as words. What features of the words are especially emphasized by the parallelisms? what features of situation? of character? How could this help us (1) interpret the ensuing dialogue and (2) summarize Jesus' meaning?

2. Analyze the parallelism of Matthew 25:34–36. What features are highlighted? How could they guide interpretation?

For other interpretive models see Fay (65–81) on parallelism in Mark 4, and Siker (76–81) on parallelism in the context of "Physician, heal yourself" (Lk 4:16–30).

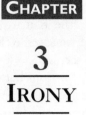

CHAPTER

3

IRONY

In many cases irony is a device of language (i.e., rhetorical), but it is not (like repetition and parallelism) a rhetorical *structure*. Language may assume a special rhetorical force when we perceive it to be incongruous with its context. And we extend the word *ironic* beyond the scope of rhetoric to describe certain situations that likewise seem incongruous in their contexts.

IRONY OF IMAGE

Ridderbos (145) points out irony in the image of the Speck and the Plank (Mt 7:3–5), in which someone with a major problem incongruously tries to correct someone else's minor problem.

> judging sinner : judged sinner = person with plank : person with speck
> with respect to (ironic) presumptuousness of offered help

There is another irony in the image of the Good Samaritan (Lk 10:25–37).

INTERPRETIVE MODEL

Bailey, 1980, 51

> The Greek text can be read, "He *brought him* to the inn," or "He *led it* (the donkey) to the inn." . . . Middle Eastern donkeys can easily carry two people, and if we

assume the first, the Samaritan is riding with the
wounded man. If we assume the second, he is acting
out the form of a servant and leading the animal to the
inn. The social distinctions between riders and leaders
of riding animals is crucial in Middle Eastern society.
Much to his surprise and humiliation, Haman (who
expects to be the rider) finds himself leading the horse
on which his enemy Mordecai is riding (Est. 6:7–11).

If a well-to-do Samaritan merchant is leading the beast that carries
the wounded man, we are looking at an *irony of situation* most
striking in the culture of the time. The Samaritan takes upon himself the form of a servant and the lawyer is told to "go and do likewise" (v 37). Donahue's comment (76) on the Unmerciful Servant
(Mt 18:23–35) notes a *verbal irony:* "In v. 34 there is a tragic irony
for the first servant in that now he will have what he originally
requested, time to pay his debt, only the time will be spent in
prison." When the servant asked for time to pay he could not know
events would give his words such bitter meaning.

We may define the essence of irony as this *contrast of knowledge and ignorance,* usually just implied in language or situation,
rather than overtly noted. In retrospect (with greater knowledge)
the servant realizes that his earlier request involved a naïve view of
the possibilities. Irony always contrasts greater and lesser knowledge; the cliché for ironic situations is "Little did they know."
Often the contrast is only implied, and sometimes it is apparent
rather than real. For example, the situational irony of the merchant
leading his donkey creates a double consciousness: we know that
such a well-to-do man is accustomed to riding, but we see him
playing the servant's part. If, however, he only seems to be ignorant of his prerogatives, then this is an example of *conscious irony*. In
the light of his final plight, the servant's request for time to pay is
clearly an example of *unconscious irony*. But it might involve

another irony of a conscious sort—if, while making his plea, the servant knew that his whole life was too short to pay the debt. Such disingenuousness has the distinct degrees of knowledge that go with irony: the servant's realistic knowledge of his plight, and the pose of ignorance which is required for his promise to pay.

Note the implication for Jesus' theme of our dependence on God's forgiveness. As formulated above (part 1.5) this analogy has just one point of resemblance: (1) below. But reflection on the first servant's language suggests at least two more points of resemblance: one arising from the conscious irony (2), and one from the unconscious (3).

> the sinner : sin = first debtor : huge debt
> with respect to (1) impossibility of propitiation
> (2) foolish optimism about propitiation
> (3) prospect of endless "payment" without propitiation

Irony is usually tacit. Skillful authors and speakers seldom draw attention to their ironies in the fashion of "Little did they know." Usually they allow their audiences the pleasure of exercising their own skill of discerning the incongruity and remarking on the irony for themselves. As a result unskillful readers may take literally what was intended ironically—and readers of the parables cannot always agree about when Jesus is being ironic. One should ask: Is it likely that he sensed an incongruity and that he thought it significant?

EXERCISE

Exercises on the Tenants (Mk 12:1–12) and the Lost Son (Lk 15:11–32)

1. Compare the tenants' words in verse 7, "This is the heir. Come, let's kill him, and the inheritance will be ours," with

the actual outcome of their plot (v 9): "The owner of the vineyard ... will come and kill those tenants and give the vineyard to others." Is this irony of language conscious or unconscious? How does it affect our understanding of Jesus' point(s) in the parable? Express your answer to this second question in one or more formulas of proportion.

2. Of the Lost Son Donahue says (157): "Rather ironically, the older son now sounds and acts very much like his brother. His understanding is also that of a slave; literally, 'he has slaved' for his father many years and apparently never even asked for a kid to celebrate. *Just as the younger son felt that the way to restore the severed relationship was to become a servant, the older brother maintained it by acting as a servant. Between the dutiful son and the prodigal is a bond much deeper than is visible on the surface.*" What are the implications of this irony for Jesus' message? Articulate them as points of resemblance that complete the following formulas.

(1) younger son : father = tax collectors and sinners : God
     with respect to ...
(2) elder son : father = Pharisees : God
     with respect to ...
(3) elder son : younger son = Pharisees : tax collectors and sinners
     with respect to ...

One could also identify and interpret many ironies of language and situation in the Unmerciful Servant (Mt 18:23–35) and the Great Supper (Lk 14:15–24).

IRONY OF CONTEXT

When Jesus' interaction with his audience creates ironies that affect the meaning of a parable, we have irony of context, as in the Lost Sheep (Lk 15:3–7).

Bailey, 1976, 147

> For the Pharisee, a "sinner" was either an immoral person who did not keep the law or a person engaged in one of the proscribed trades, among which was herding sheep. . . .
>
> Any man who believed shepherds were unclean would naturally be offended if addressed as one. Yet Jesus begins, "Which one of *you* having a hundred sheep . . . does not he leave. . . ." Thus this beginning can be understood as an indirect and yet very powerful attack on the Pharisaic attitudes toward proscribed professions. To show deference to their feelings in this matter he would have had to begin the parable something like this: "Which man of you owning a hundred sheep, if he heard that the hired shepherd had lost one, would he not summon the shepherd and demand that the sheep be found under threat of fine?"

This same conflict with the Pharisees creates similar ironies in the Two Debtors (Lk 7:36–50) and the Places at Table (Lk 14:7–11). In the latter case Jesus assumes a pose of sympathy with the motives of the guests who jockey for "places of honor" (v 7). "If you really want respect," he is saying, "take the dramatic approach. Let your host find that you have taken a place far beneath your dignity, and let everyone be impressed when he gives you a place of distinction." The guests' logic is pushed to its shameful absurdity. The analogy (*parabolē*, v 7) conveys both his warning (v 11a) and his recommendation (v 11b).

(1) affected humility : host's response = true humility :
    God's response
with respect to resulting honor

(2) social presumption : host's response = spiritual pre-
    sumption : God's response
with respect to resulting humiliation

At least one parable exemplifies *narrative* irony, a kind that preachers retelling familiar stories sometimes use as follows: "When the father called for fine clothes and a feast the prodigal said, 'No, no! You musn't make such a fuss. No party, please.'—But that's not right, is it? He accepted the celebration." Just so, after setting up the hypothetical situation of the Friend at Midnight, Jesus narrates, apparently with a straight face, an outcome that his hearers knew was socially inconceivable (Lk 11:7): "Then the one inside answers, 'Don't bother me. The door is already locked, and my children are with me in bed. I can't get up and give you any-thing.'" Bailey's research justifies this ironic reading.

INTERPRETIVE MODEL

Bailey, 1976, 124

> Jesus is saying, "Can you imagine ... silly excuses about sleeping children and a barred door?" The Orien-tal listener/reader knows the communal responsibility for the guest and responds, "No, we cannot imagine it."

Jesus' rhetoric is the soberfaced, ironic description of a ridiculous outcome. So too his story of the master who would "say to the ser-vant when he comes in from the field, 'Come along now and sit down to eat'" (Lk 17:7); Jesus' hearers know better.

EXERCISE

Exercise on the Good Samaritan (Lk 10:25–37)

Both the story-image of this parable and Jesus' encounter with the lawyer have many ironies. Describe as many as you can, with a view to enhancing your understanding of Jesus' message to the lawyer and Luke's message to his reader.

See also Ireland (305–7) on the Unjust Steward (Lk 16:1–13).

PARADOX

Paradox is the irony of apparent contradiction that really has coherent significance. Gundry describes an example of paradox in the metaphorical analogy of Burying the Dead (Mt 8:21–22).

INTERPRETIVE MODEL

Gundry, 153

> The command to "let the dead bury their own dead" may mean that the spiritually dead (cf. Luke 15:24, 32; John 5:24; Eph 2:1) should be left to bury the physically dead. Alternatively, the statement refers only to the physically dead and is laden with irony: "Let those who have been dead for some time bury those who have just died." Impossible? Yes, and in the very impossibility lies an irony that implies, "Let the business take care of itself—it is no concern of yours."

EXERCISE

Exercise on the Grain of Wheat (Jn 12:20–26; cf. Lot's Wife, Lk 17:32–33)

Describe what it is that creates a paradox in Jesus' vehicle—the buried seed that springs to life—as a way of explicating the spiritual paradox of his tenor.

OVERSTATEMENT AND UNDERSTATEMENT

Rhetorical exaggeration in *hyperbole* and understatement in *meiosis* are special kinds of irony; we know better than to take them at face value. Among Jesus' more celebrated hyperboles are the image of the Speck and Plank (Mt 7:3–5) and his preface to the Unmerciful Servant (Mt 18:22) enjoining Peter to forgive his brother "seventy-seven times" (or "seventy times seven"). Some critics have concluded that tradition or the evangelist must have attached the latter parable to Peter's question because he asks "how often?" while the parable tells "how much." But Jesus' answer is deliberately inapposite; one shouldn't count offenses. Understood as ironic, "seventy-seven times" implies as much; the parable answers the question that Peter should have asked.

One remarkable detail of the Unjust Judge (Lk 18:1–8) is perhaps an instance of meiosis. One would think that Jesus' question, "When the Son of Man comes, will he find faith on the earth?" ought to be a rhetorical question. Of course there will be faith on the earth! But coming at the end it sounds instead like a real question, thus seeming to understate the likelihood. We are prodded into taking the question more seriously and pondering on the need for persistence in faith and prayer that otherwise we might take for granted. Meiosis clearly reflects a hearer's mind and heart in the lawyer's response to Jesus' question, "Which of these three do you think was a neighbor to the man who fell into the hands of robbers?" (Lk 10:36). He understates things outrageously with his mere "The one who showed mercy on him." He manages to reply correctly while ignoring the special circumstances of a Samaritan's charity toward a Jew.

See also Holmgren (252–60) on the Pharisee and Publican (Lk 18:9–14).

RHETORICAL QUESTIONS

A rhetorical question implies that any fool can answer. Since we know the question is unnecessary, it is therefore ironic. So it is in the Rich Fool (Lk 12:13–21).

INTERPRETIVE MODEL

Scott, 137

> The perception of limited goods underlies the wisdom tradition's demand to share wealth. If one person hoards wealth, there will be none left to go around. If there is surplus today, there must be shortage tomorrow, so the rich man's saving up of his harvest to provide only for his own comfort offends against the community's possibilities, wastes God's gifts, and ensures the impoverishment of others....
>
> God's question "Whose will they be?" leads the audience to the appropriate response: "Those for whom they were originally intended."

As Scott's observations imply, to interpret a rhetorical question we identify: (a) the point at issue, (b) the particular audience whose assent is expected, and (c) the practical response that this audience should make. This story ends abruptly with a reply from the Fool (is he simply dumbfounded or already struck dead?), so that the question is tossed out to Jesus' audience—including the disappointed heir whose request prompted this parable of rebuke (v 13).

Hunter (54–55) notes a similar dynamic in the Two Sons (Mt 21:28–32).

> Invited to pass judgment on a simple story, the Scribes and Pharisees find, like King David, that "the story pops up and leaves them flat." For before they quite know what they are saying, they are admitting that penitent publicans and prostitutes are nearer to God's grace than professing churchmen who ignore his call.

We should note, however, that Jesus' analogy no doubt still failed to persuade the scribes and Pharisees of his point—that "the tax collectors and the prostitutes are entering the kingdom of God ahead of you"—since immediately after this encounter they "looked for a way to arrest him" (21:46). Why should they admit that *they* are "professing churchmen who ignore [God's] call"? Unlike David (2Sa 12:13), they are not convicted of sin. By itself a rhetorical question's appeal to the obvious may not persuade a hostile audience that Jesus is right.

Exercise on the Murdered Galileans, the Victims of Siloam, and the Barren Fig Tree (Lk 13:1–9)

Each analogy in this triplet of warnings contains a rhetorical question. Why does Jesus answer the first two himself (vv 2–3, 4–5)? What truth is emphasized by the third question, "Why should it use up the soil?" (v 7)? What response does the owner expect from the vinedresser? How does the story exploit this expectation and help to sharpen Jesus' implied warning? For further practice, study the effects of rhetorical questions in the Friend at Midnight (Lk 11:5–8), the Lost Sheep (Mt 18:12–14), and the Tenants (Mt 21:33–46).

INAPPOSITE ANSWERS

When people's questions imply false assumptions, Jesus either refuses to answer (e.g., his silence before Herod in Lk 23:9), or reframes the terms of the question (e.g., his response concerning the man born blind in Jn 9:2–3): "His disciples asked him, 'Rabbi, who sinned, this man or his parents, that he was born blind?' Jesus answered, 'Neither this man nor his parents sinned, but this happened so that the work of God might be displayed in his life.'" This irony of a deliberately *inapposite answer* turns up in the Good Samaritan (Lk 10:25–37).

INTERPRETIVE MODEL

Funk, 1966, 221

> With respect to the Lucan context, . . . Jesus does not
> allow the lawyer's question (and ours) to dominate the
> parable, for the lawyer's question is an effort to hold the
> question of neighbor at arm's length, and hence the
> force of the commandment. From the perspective of the
> parable the question "Who is my neighbor?" is an
> impossible question. The disjunction between question
> and answer, considered so grievous by Jülicher and
> those who have followed him, far from being inimical
> to the parable, is necessary to the point. This means also
> that Jesus does not allow the law to dominate love as
> God's drawing near. Rather, Jesus proclaims the law in
> a context qualified by the event of divine love and inter-
> prets it with the help of the concrete instance of love's
> needfulness.

Funk first describes the lack of correspondence between the
lawyer's question and Jesus' response, showing what it is that makes
the answer inapposite. Then he justifies his interpretation of the
parable by stating the significance of Jesus' challenge to the lawyer's
expectations.

EXERCISE

Exercise on the Rich Fool (Lk 12:13–21)

Use Funk's two steps to deal with Jesus' response (in both the
story of the parable and his commentary on it) to the request of
the man in the crowd (v 13): "Teacher, tell my brother to divide
the inheritance with me."

4
PLOT

Most of Jesus' parables add some narrative features such as plot, character, and setting to the essential analogy. In turning to narrative we are not turning away from diction and rhetoric, for they are decisive factors in our understanding of all the other elements that make a story.

NARRATIVE SELECTION

The parables are so familiar that everything may seem inevitable; characters, events, and outcomes assume classic shapes. Variants that Jesus could have chosen instead may not occur to us; and yet *narrative choices*—an author's decisions about what to include—are significant cues to meaning. Why does Jesus omit the outcome of the Barren Fig Tree (Lk 13:6–9)? Why pay the vineyard laborers in reverse order (Mt 20:8)? Why give talents or pounds to three servants or ten rather than to one good and one bad (Mt 25:15; Lk 19:13)? The less obvious the question, the more fruitful it may be. Some of Jesus' situations and plots recur commonly in storytelling, and others' versions can prod us into discovering such questions. Thus Jeremias (32) quotes from the Midrash on Canticles 4:12 an analogue to Jesus' parable of the Hidden Treasure (Mt 13:44).

> The situation described in Cant. 4.12 ... is like a man who inherited a place full of rubbish.

The inheritor was lazy and he sold it for a ridiculously small sum.

The purchaser dug therein industriously and found in it a treasure.

He built therewith a great palace and passed through the bazaar with a train of slaves whom he had bought with the treasure. When the seller saw it he could have choked himself (with vexation).

Jeremias comments: "The audience expected that the story of the treasure in the field would be about a splendid palace which the finder built, or a train of slaves with whom he promenades through the bazaar." This story helps us notice that Jesus said nothing about the treasure's use. This silence could mean that the kingdom is an end in itself, not a means for other ends—a theme perhaps implied in Jeremias's description of Jesus' point: the "overwhelming experience of the splendour of [the] discovery" (201).

Such an *unexpected resolution* may hint at Jesus' purposes. So Beare notes (193–94) even in the very simple saying of the Two Ways (Mt 7:13–14). Another instructive instance is the Palestinian Talmud story (quoted in part 3.1) of Bar Maayan, which Jeremias (178) believes was known to Jesus and his audience. As an analogue to the Wedding Feast (Mt 22:1–14) and the Great Supper (Lk 14:15–24) it is illuminating.

INTERPRETIVE MODEL

Scott, 172

The Bar Maayan parable is told to illustrate the one good deed the man did during his life so as to account for his good burial:

He never did a meritorious deed in his life. But one time he made a banquet for the councillors of his town but they did not come. He said, "Let the poor come and eat the food, so that it not go to waste."

In this story the councilors were justified in dishonoring the host because he was a publican and therefore a sinner. But his response—his vengeance on those who dishonored him—points to the appropriate social response, a snub. . . . The response of the man [in Jesus' parable] is similar to that of Bar Maayan: he sends his servant to collect the poor. Yet there are two important differences. In the Bar Maayan story the action is an example of a good deed. Bar Maayan feeds the poor. No such purpose is at stake here. Second, Bar Maayan is a publican, a sinner. In terms of honor, his proper place is with the poor. The point of the Bar Maayan story is to show how such a wicked one could ever receive the honor of a good burial in the first place. Here no honor redounds to the man. Since he is anonymous we do not know whether he had sufficient honor to issue the invitations. Now his fate rests with those he has invited. He belongs with the poor, with those who dwell along the streets. In order to insult those originally invited, he loses his place of honor.

We need no alternate versions of a folkmotif to be fairly sure that the audience normally expected a story to end with a resolution—a *denouement* (French for "unravelling") of the complications that make the plot. In cases of *suspended resolution* we should ask why Jesus stops before the story is finished.

EXERCISE

Exercises on the Lost Son (Lk 15:11–32), the Tenants (Mk 12:1–12), and the Barren Fig Tree (Lk 13:6–9)

1. What does Jesus' message to the Pharisees in the whole parable of the Lost Son (Lk 15:1–2) gain by his omitting the elder son's response to his father's plea (vv 31–32)?

2. Why does Jesus express the fate of the tenants (Mk 12:9), not as an accomplished fact, but as a hypothesis about the future?

3. Why does Jesus not tell us what happens to the barren fig tree?

An *unmotivated action* may be a cue to the meaning of a parable. If a character does something for no apparent reason, perhaps Jesus had a reason for including it, as in the Vineyard Laborers (Mt 20:1–16).

INTERPRETIVE MODEL

Gundry, 399

> Because the grumbling centers on the amount of payment, not on the order of payment, some argue that the parable did not originally illustrate the reversal of first and last, but only divine generosity. Without the reversal in order of payment, however, the grumbling—a major feature of the parable—would never have occurred. Thus the reversal is as important as the grumbling it makes possible.

Why make the workers be paid in reverse order of their hiring? Some exegetes say Matthew added this to justify (however speciously) his addition of verse 16 as the point of the parable. But Gundry shows that the detail is a narrative necessity, though the story gives the owner no motive. If the all-day workers were sent home first, each with his denarius, they could not see the one-hour workers receive a denarius too, or expect more for themselves, or make the complaint that elicits the owner's response and Jesus' point. This inference strengthens Gundry's case for the theme of "first and last."

A psychologically unlikely motivation or an *implausible action* may also be a signpost to Jesus' intent. Why should a king freely remit such a huge debt as in the Unmerciful Servant (Mt 18:23–35)? Why should a father receive so kindly such a wastrel as the Lost Son (Lk 15:11–32)? (Hunter [63] suggests that a real father might kill the son sooner than the fatted calf.) What is impossible with a man, or at least unlikely, is possible with God—and in both cases that is Jesus' point exactly. In general "the atypical features [are] Jesus' usual way of revealing the unworldly character of the coming kingdom of God" (Huffman, 219). When some implausibility in the story distorts the reality of the "real world," we should look for the possibility of a special marker of Jesus' meaning.

Special markers may be found in details of a parable that are socially or morally embarrassing, such as Jeremias observes in the unjust steward and judge and the "despised shepherd" (179). Though the deception in the Hidden Treasure (Mt 13:44) is a potential distraction from Jesus' point, it can help us find that point, if we ask why he made a narrative choice so likely to distract.

INTERPRETIVE MODEL

Sider, 1984, 371

> The purchase is deceptive because of the suppressed discrepancy between the price paid for the field and the value of the field and treasure thus acquired. Why was that feature introduced at all? ... What could the discrepancy *in itself* have to do with the kingdom? The answer suggested in the following equation involves themes at least as old in interpretation as Calvin. ...
>
> price of field < value of treasure = all a human can do < riches of grace
>
> Why did Jesus not avoid the ethical problem entirely, by having the man find the treasure on his own property, as in some versions of the tradition? If the treasure were gained thus it would cost him nothing: therefore,

perhaps, Jesus wished to include the idea of total commitment. Even then, why did Jesus not avoid the ethical problem by having the man pay a fair price for field and treasure together? The treasure of the kingdom is a gift of grace, not something we deserve—such as would be depicted by a man capable of paying full value for the treasure. In this parable Jesus evidently wished to say at least two things about the kingdom. First, it comes of God's grace, not of our ability: this requires that the purchase be a notable bargain. Second, the kingdom demands total commitment: this requires that the man pay with everything he has.

Jesus would hardly permit a deception to create such a moral distraction unless he could not avoid it and still make his points. The features of the story that combine to create the distraction are probably the vehicles of the points he intends to make.

(1) finder : profit in purchase = believer : grace of kingdom
with respect to gain beyond one's means

(2) finder's sacrifice : treasure = believer's sacrifice :
kingdom
with respect to "selling all" for the gain

Very ordinary narrative choices can be significant too. If the Sower (Mk 4:3–8) existed only for the sake of the contrast between the risk of a crop failure and the actuality of abundant harvest, as Jeremias says (150–51), there would be no reason for Jesus' choosing to distinguish and describe three unfruitful soils. If God's mercy to sinners were the sole point of the Lost Son (Lk 15:11–32), as some have maintained, Jesus would hardly have chosen to give the elder son's episode such an elaborate form. Not everything in a parable necessarily has a thematic function, but it can't hurt to ask about everything.

A story is a series of forks in the road. A *spontaneously responding audience* is little conscious of any possibilities but the ones presented—except in serial fictions like the television soaps, which between episodes allow one to expect or desire one twist of the plot rather than another. This leisure is just what the *reflective interpreter* needs, to consider systematically all the roads not taken. Thus Crossan cites Midrashic and Talmudic analogues for the Hidden Treasure (Mt 13:44).

INTERPRETIVE MODEL

Crossan, 1979, 61, 74–75

The minimal tree diagram necessary to furnish the plot options of these Jewish treasure parables is given [in the next figure].

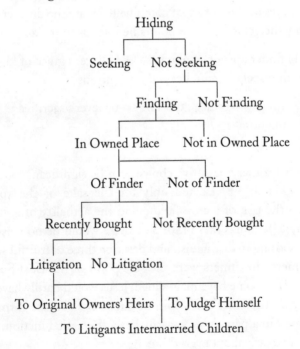

[The first two plot elements—Hiding and Not Seeking—are very familiar in Jewish stories, but with Finding in Another's Land,] Jesus' story has suddenly taken a very significant turn. . . .

The plot option chosen by Jesus at this point may be underlined by comparing it with a treasure story from the Roman world as recorded both by Horace around 30 B.C.E. and Porphyrio of Tyre (232–304 C.E.). . . . This diagram shows that there were three options possible for Jesus' story at this motifemic decision. The Finding could have been: (a) Not in Owned Place; (b) In Owned Place, but of Finder; (c) In Owned Place, but Not Of Finder.

Crossan identifies further choices of plot elements or "motifemes" as "Rehiding" (77), "Selling All One Has" (79), and "Buying the Field" (81)—both necessary preliminaries to Jesus' outcome, possessing the treasure. Some of these options we might notice anyway, but the diagram keeps us from oversights. The more versions of a story we have, the fuller our diagrams. But even without research in folklore such as Crossan's, we can diagram Jesus' narrative choices through any parable.

EXERCISE

Exercise on the Lost Son (Lk 15:11–32)

Make a tree diagram of Jesus' narrative choices and alternatives for his characters' *actions,* from the younger son's request for his inheritance, to the elder son's options as created by his father's appeal (vv 31–32). Which choices have the farthest-reaching consequences for the course of the story? Why? Which choices seem to have the most significance for Jesus' message to the Pharisees about the tax collectors and sinners (15:1–2)? Why?

See also Stein (126) on the Vineyard Laborers (Mt 20:1–16).

NARRATIVE CLIMAX

Any feature of narrative order may be an important cue for interpretation, such as Gundry notes (426–27) in the Tenants (Mt 21:33–46). Our normal expectation is that the order of events in a narrative image will correspond to any chronological significance of the tenor. For example, because God's mercy to repentant sinners is the Pharisees' source of dissatisfaction (Lk 15:1–2), the elder son complains about his brother after his return, not before. Kistemaker (12) appeals to this consideration in preferring the second of two possible understandings of the Children in the Marketplace (Mt 11:16–19; Lk 7:31–35).

(1) Jews : John and Jesus = children refusing to play : children suggesting games

with respect to uniform uncooperativeness about contrasting invitations

(2) Jews : John and Jesus = children suggesting games : children refusing to play

with respect to contrary expectations

"The children who suggest the glad and sad games of wedding and funeral," he says, "are the Jews who want John to be merry and Jesus to mourn" because this reading "places the complaints of the children applied to John and Jesus in a chronological order."

The ordering of a story's *climactic* elements is especially interesting. It makes a difference which of the four soils in the Sower (Mk 4:3–8) is mentioned last. Ancients and moderns alike expect a climax at the end of a narrative series, as Hunter notes (53) in the successive commissions of the Vineyard Laborers (Mt 20:1–16).

This parable excellently illustrates the 'rule of end stress', for the spotlight falls on the employer's astonishing generosity to the eleventh hour labourers which provokes the indignant protest of those who had worked the whole day.

The point turns on the contrast in the payment of the all-day and eleventh-hour workers. Nothing at all is said of the reaction of those who were hired at the hours between; they are included partly to make the latest hiring somewhat more plausible, but mostly to create the series which builds to the story's climactic surprise: those who worked least received as much as those who worked most.

Hunter says (11): "Stories become more effective if you follow certain rough rules in telling them ... [such as] 'the rule of three', whereby the story has three main characters ('An Englishman, an Irishman, and a Scotsman ...')." He shows how a series of three characters and episodes prepares the climax in the Talents (Mt 25:14–30).

INTERPRETIVE MODEL

Hunter, 81

> In parables with three characters like this one, the spotlight falls, by the rule of "end stress," on the third character in the story—that is, on the servant who did nothing with his money. Whom did this "barren rascal" signify in the mind of Jesus? (The successful two, be it noted, are only there as foils to him.) Who was this "slothful and wicked servant" whose caution amounted to a breach of trust? The answer is that he typified the pious Pharisee who hoarded the light God gave him (the Law) and kept for himself what was meant for mankind. Such a policy of selfish exclusivism yields God no interest on his capital; it is tantamount to defrauding him and must incur his judgment. And the time for settling accounts is approaching.

Hunter finds Jesus' point in the last person's situation. Sometimes we count episodes rather than characters. Scott (272) observes that though we have only two *characters* in the Unmerciful Servant (Mt 18:23–35), there are three distinct *episodes* of guilt and judgment that create a deeply moving climax: (1) sentence on the first servant is passed but reversed; (2) sentence on the second servant is passed and executed; therefore, (3) sentence on the first servant is confirmed and executed.

EXERCISE

Exercise on the Rich Man and Lazarus (Lk 16:19–31)

If we choose the rule of end stress as our guide, what would be Jesus' main point in this parable? Does the preceding context (16:14–17) tend to support this conclusion or undercut it?

Our anticipation of a narrative climax may be exploited rather than simply fulfilled, as in the case of the Wedding Feast (Mt 22:1–14) and Great Supper (Lk 14:15–24). Scott says (170): "Since the excuses form a triad, a hearer would expect the third invitation to be accepted. . . . This violation of the triadic expectation underscores the totality of the rejection." The rule of three leads us to expect a contrasting third party, as in The Three Little Pigs or Goldilocks and the Three Bears. But this is a party where *nobody* came; Jesus makes his hearers not just know, but feel, what rejecting God's call means.

The climax of the Good Samaritan (Lk 10:29–37) is unexpected too.

INTERPRETIVE MODEL

Scott, 198

> The Samaritan's appearance in the story is indeed surprising, for the expected triad is priest, Levite, and Israelite, . . . a threefold division of the Jewish people. . . . The Mishnah evidences the hierarchical character of the formula:

A priest precedes a levite, a levite an Israelite, an Israelite a bastard, a bastard a *Nathin,* a *Nathin* a proselyte, and a proselyte a freed slave. This applies when all are [otherwise] equal; but if a bastard is learned in the Law and a High Priest is ignorant of the Law, the bastard that is learned in the Law precedes the High Priest that is ignorant of the Law.

In this example the threefold formula provides the main divisions of respectable Jewish society. Somewhat in the way of our parable, a scandalous comparison is introduced. An ignorant high priest is less than a learned bastard.

Jesus' hearers expect a clerical/lay contrast in the third character; he hits them with an unexpected order of contrast. The question "Who is my neighbor?" has tacitly introduced excuses for avoiding charity, but Jesus says, in effect, that a slack priest (or lawyer) is less than a caring half-breed.

EXERCISE

Exercise on the Talents (Mt 25:14–30)

In order to appreciate the narrative functions of the second servant in this parable, try imagining it without him. How does the formulaic *repetition* of "Master ... you entrusted me with *n* talents ..." and "Well done ..." affect our expectation of the third encounter, when we already know what the last servant has done with his talent? How does it influence our response to his explanation and to the master's response?

See also Kloppenborg (477ff.) on the Unjust Steward (Lk 16:1–8).

Though the argumentation of Jesus' analogies appeals to the intellect, a story's climax moves the emotions. Like other literature, the parables frequently reach our minds through our feelings: by connotations, attractive and repulsive characters, and many other features in addition to climactic ordering. In our quest for the reflective and doctrinal content of Jesus' message we may neglect the significance of our emotions and those of Jesus' characters and first audience, unless we make a habit of asking, about each feature of a parable, "How does this make one think *and* feel?"

COMIC AND TRAGIC PLOT PATTERNS

Often we can sense, long before the end of a story, that it is shaping up to a happy or an unhappy ending. Such expectations contribute to comic and tragic moods; we laugh at mistaken marital jealousy in Shakespeare's *Merry Wives of Windsor*, but weep at it in *Othello*, partly because we foresee in the one situation restored harmony and understanding, but murder in the other. The shape of the plot, then, is a major factor in the emotional effect of a story.

Although many of Jesus' hearers certainly never attended a theater, they would still be moved by the comic or tragic trend of a plot, because these things are much like archetypal images (cf. part 3.1), transcending the cultural boundaries between Jew and Greek. The tragic pattern appears in the Unmerciful Servant (Mt 18:23–35).

INTERPRETIVE MODEL

Via, 141–42

> In the opening crisis it had not occurred to the servant that the debt might be cancelled. He thought in terms of claims made and claims paid, and pleaded for time to make his payment. He must have known that he could not really have followed through, but in his extremity he was grasping for straws. Because he at least did not place the blame for his plight on someone else, we are prepared to be sympathetic with him. Our

sympathy recoils, however, when we witness his behavior in part two. His understanding of human relationships ... had been challenged but not altered by the mercy shown him. At the end he still had not come to recognize what mercy does and had to be told—after it was too late—what he should have grasped on his own and what the consequence of his failure would be....

The final physical isolation of the unforgiving servant from his lord and from his fellow servants only confirms the estrangement from others which was implicit in his self-understanding from the beginning and which was never shattered.

Via starts by noting the story's promising prospects; in the first episode the servant's new lease on life creates hopeful expectations. As things turn out, however, it is not the movement of comedy, but an example of the ironic semblance of good fortune that generally precedes the catastrophe of a tragedy. Via also identifies characteristic features of Greek tragedy. One is the tragic choice that brings the servant to a bad end in spite of his prospects: because he is committed to the principle of fair payment, he cannot accept grace—this is his tragic flaw. His missed moment of recognition and transformation, as Via shows, comes when not even the king's forgiveness—the means of his own surprising good fortune—allows him to witness the workings of mercy. His doom in prison is isolation as bad as death—a tragic fate.

Not every feature of Greek tragedy was necessarily on the minds of Jesus' hearers. But sometimes he told stories about people whose moral actions brought them to a bad end, and all such stories involve the features that Via notes. For Jesus' moral derelicts act wrongly because of flawed character, distorted vision, and misguided choices. And their isolation reflects the separation of bad from good that pervades his teaching: e.g., the Sower, the Weeds, the Net (Mt 13); the Wedding Feast and Wedding Garment (Mt

22); the Ten Maidens, the Talents, the Sheep and Goats (Mt 25). The response of Jesus' audience to a story of hopeful prospects overcome by human depravity must have resembled what Aristotle describes in *Poetics;* within limits, his categories help us determine how Jesus' tragic narratives work upon the emotions of his audience. Via (143) rightly treats the unforgiving servant as a negative example of a positive fact: God's forgiveness, when truly received, enables ours—even makes it inevitable. How does he discover this truth in the parable? By responding to the very tragic features that he identifies. They embody the tragic crisis of the servant's perverse choice: the king's forgiveness should have enabled his but did not.

Few parables, however, have a purely tragic plot pattern: the Rich Fool (Lk 12:13–21), the Tenants (Mk 12:1–12), the Unmerciful Servant (Mt 18:23–35), and the Wedding Garment (Mt 22:11–14). Few have purely comic plot patterns: the Unjust Judge (Lk 18:1–8), the Hidden Treasure and the Pearl (Mt 13:44–46), the Lost Sheep and the Lost Coin (Lk 15:1–10), and the Unjust Steward (Lk 16:1–13). In some, the action is too inconsequential to be counted—e.g., the Mustard Seed and Leaven (Mt 13:30–33), the Patched Garment and Wineskins (Mk 2:21–22)—and the Barren Fig Tree (Lk 13:6–9) suspends the outcome.

Most parables have two outcomes: a happy ending for the good characters and an unhappy one for the bad. In this respect the Sower (Mk 4:3–8), the Vineyard Laborers (Mt 20:1–16), the Two Sons (Mt 21:28–32), and the Good Samaritan (Lk 10:25–37) are like Shakespeare's *Much Ado About Nothing, Twelfth Night, The Tempest*, and *2 Henry IV,* where the estrangement of unrepentant antagonists or outsiders (Don John, Malvolio, Antonio, and Falstaff) is a more or less incidental coloring to a mainly happy ending. In the Lost Son (Lk 15:11–32), however, the unresolved antagonism of the elder son is not just a detail. More of Jesus' story-length parables are like Aristotle's "tragedy of double outcome," where the doom of evil characters sets the tone of the end, despite the happiness of the good: thus the Two Builders (Mt 7:24–27), the Great Supper (Lk 14:15–24), the Wedding Feast (Mt 22:1–14), the Talents (Mt 25:14–30), the Pounds (Lk 19:11–27), the Pharisee and Publican (Lk 18:9–14), the Rich Man and Lazarus (Lk 16:19–31). People talk about Sophocles' tragic "world" and Shakespeare's comic "world," but they must have known that the one real world is not so simple. Thus it is in Jesus' symbolic depiction of the spiritual world in most story-parables, as also in analogies like the Servant in Authority (Mt 24:45–51) and the Sheep and Goats (Mt 25:31–46).

Jeremias (179–80) describes this mixed effect in the accepted and rejected guests of the Great Supper. Likewise, he observes (175) of the Ten Maidens: "Only he who pays attention to the note of joy on which the parable starts (v. 1) is able to grasp the stern warning it conveys: all the more let it be your concern to prepare yourself for the hour of trial and judgement that will precede the fulfilment." The very plot structure confirms Jesus' resolute division of humanity into friend and foe (e.g., Mt 12:30; cf. Lk 11:23): "He who is not with me is against me, and he who does not gather with me scatters."

Via's insightful comments (164–67) on the Lost Son (Lk 15:11–32) exemplify many possibilities for using the comic pattern to illuminate some of the parables. Comparing this story with the prevailing pattern of comic plots shows us something more than an audience's expectations; we can read several significant features of Jesus' message in his choice of a special brand of comic plot. First, there is meaning in the particular sort of conflict that complicates this plot. The complication of a comedy generally means big trouble. It may look deadly to the protagonist; "despair" is not too strong a word for the prodigal's lowest state. But his plight is not "tragic" because there is no catastrophe. Even as light a play as Shakespeare's *A Midsummer Night's Dream* confronts

Hermia with death both in the city (1.1.65) and in the woods (2.2.156). The prodigal makes his own trouble, Via says, by his unwarranted dissatisfaction and his recklessness. No devil makes him do it. In Milton's *Paradise Lost* God foresees that Adam and Eve may blame "Thir maker, or thir making, or thir Fate," but such exterior sources of trouble, though common in comedy, are irrelevant to Jesus' comic progress of the human soul according to its inner choices.

Second, as Via observes (166), the progress of this plot "from a society controlled by habit, bondage, or law ... to a society marked by freedom" reflects the nature of the gospel another way. The lost son's new knowledge of himself means that his place at home does not depend on his own exertions. There was one moment of discovery among the pigs, but since the prodigal's new plan was to reestablish his position *by his own efforts* as a hired servant, the greater discovery came when his father unexpectedly received him without reservation as a son—a position he could not gain by merit or effort.

Third, there is significance in this parable's version of the ritual festivity of comedy. In the ecstatic Dionysian tradition of the Greeks the common comic suspension of ordinary morality could extend to spectacular and revolting excesses. By contrast, the celebration of the prodigal's return is ecstatic but not Dionysian; it is hilarious and decorous at once. Here the comic mode shows the influence of the biblical insistence upon the responsibility that should go with freedom. The celebration also intimates that banqueting is a Jewish symbol for the messianic consummation of all things precisely because it is an archetype of happy endings.

Fourth, the bound society characteristic of the antagonist in comedy neatly fits Jesus' purpose for the elder son as an analogy for the Pharisees (Lk 15:1–2). Legalism is his motive; his notions of social order make him antisocial. The prodigal made his own trouble; his brother troubles himself most.

Fifth, as Frye has observed (35), what resolves the typical comic plot is the restoration of a social circle. The ending of this parable is untypical because the family circle is still broken, not by the prodigal's prodigality or the father's just cause for resentment, but by the elder brother's refusal—on his misguided principles—to join the party. Here the comic pattern is influenced by the Pharisees' misunderstanding of biblical grace.

EXERCISE

Exercises on the Rich Fool (Lk 12:13–21), the Tenants (Mt 21:33–46; Mk 12:1–12; Lk 20:9–19), and the Good Samaritan (Lk 10:25–37)

1. Examine the plot pattern of the Rich Fool. What does the man do with his opportunity for recognition and transformation? Why?

2. To feel the foreboding tone of genuine tragedy an audience must expect disaster. To see how the mere description of the making of the vineyard (v 1) creates this foreboding in the Tenants, compare it with the Song of Isaiah that it echoes (Is 5:1–4, and especially 5–7). From this foreknowledge of the audience, what ironies arise as the wicked tenants miss their opportunities for recognition and transformation? Jesus' hearers must have expected the tragic outcome as part of the story. How does he exploit that expectation? With what effects for tone and theme?

3. The Good Samaritan proceeds to a happy ending but its manifestations of the typical comic plot pattern are markedly different from what we have seen in the Lost Son. Describe the essentials of this version of the comic plot. How does Jesus exploit his audience's ordinary expectations? What do his narrative choices suggest about his purposes?

Other narrative features of the parables, more than we can study in detail, have significant emotional force. How does *suspense* contribute to the effect of the Talents (Mt 25:14–30)? In the Weeds (Mt 13:24–30, 36–43), what do the the roles of farmer as *protago-nist* and enemy as *antagonist* contribute to our feelings, and thereby to Jesus' message? How does the *reversal* of characters' fortunes affect us in the Unmerciful Servant (Mt 18:23–35), the Ten Maid-ens (Mt 25:1–13), and the Pharisee and Publican (Lk 18:9–14)?

NARRATIVE PROPORTION

Another cue to meaning is the proportions of space and time given to components of a plot, such as the proportions of the Sower.

INTERPRETIVE MODEL

Stein, 113

> The parable of the soils (MARK 4:3–9) ... has fre-quently been interpreted as an encouragement and assurance to the disciples that the kingdom of God had indeed come and, "in spite of every failure and opposi-tion, from hopeless beginnings, God brings forth the triumphant end which he had promised." There are sev-eral reasons, however, for questioning this interpretation which rejects the canonical interpretation of the para-ble found in MARK 4:14–20. For one, it would appear that the amount of space devoted in this parable to the other three soils (vs. 3–7) cannot be ignored. In contrast to a single verse devoted to the good soil, we have five verses devoted to the other soils. This seems to be an inordinate amount of space to devote simply to the stage setting or "local coloring" of the parable's main point. Furthermore it should be noted that the average length of each of the first three soils is actually greater than the length of the description of the good soil!

In such brief and economical stories as the narrative parables, Jesus will not ramble on about something without a thematic purpose. This matter of *pacing* can guide interpretation in other ways. As Stein says (126) of the Vineyard Laborers (Mt 20:1–16), "In the conclusion of the parable the paying of the third-, sixth-, and ninth-hour workers is simply eliminated since they are unimportant for the point of the parable." Here the criterion of pacing corroborates the evidence of end stress (as already noted, "Narrative Climax") in support of the view that Jesus' point in the parable depends mainly on the owner's treatment of the eleventh-hour workers.

EXERCISE

Exercise on the Tenants (Mt 21:33–46; Mk 12:1–12; Lk 20:9–19)

In this parable considerations of pacing and proportion converge with the phenomena of climax and with the "rule of three." Jeremias suggests (71–72) that, of the three varying synoptic accounts of servants sent to the vineyard, Luke's version is closest to Jesus' original because it comes closest to the rule of three: two servants beaten, a third wounded. Mark, he says, has "abandoned the popular triple formula" with his "multitude of servants, some of whom are beaten and some killed"; and in Matthew "the climax, as we find it in Mark and Luke, is completely spoilt. He starts with the sending out of a number of servants, some of whom are ill-treated, some killed, and some stoned. Then follows a further mission, more numerous than the first, whose fate is the same." But we cannot confine Jesus to the simple folk-story triplet. (Not even Luke exemplifies it, with his three servants followed by the son.) Where we find a departure from the formula we should look for another pattern. Mark's initial climax of three (the beating, head wound, and death) is the first member of a larger climax: three servants, many servants, the son.

1. i   (v 3) They took him and beat him
   ii (v 4) They wounded him in the head
   iii (v 5a) Him they killed
2.   (v 5b) So with many others
3.   (v 7) "This is the heir. Come, let's kill him."

Keeping in mind that stoning was the special penalty for religious apostasy (Gundry says that "the tenant farmers treated the servants as false prophets" [426]), look in Matthew's version for a variant form of Mark's combination of climaxes. Analyze it with an outline. What does this structure signify for Jesus' message to the chief priests and Pharisees (vv 40–44)? for their response (vv 45–46)?

5
CHARACTER

Many of Jesus' characters are "characters" who invite us to think of them as distinctive—even unique—human beings. We need to study all the details of language, action, and circumstance which indicate Jesus' *characterizations,* that is, his delineation of characters' traits. This is simpler, of course, than characterization in modern drama and fiction, where characters can be literary ends. Neither plot nor character is an end in itself in Jesus' parables, but means to his theme, as *vehicle* implies. Even though we find no complex psychological studies, Jesus' treatment of motives and relationships may be subtle and evocative. Though "adjectives like 'good' or 'bad,' 'wise' or 'foolish' do not make us look into the soul of the characters" (Gerhardsson, 331), their words and actions can, as in Via's perceptive analysis of the picaresque Unjust Steward (159–61).

CUES TO CHARACTERIZATION

As soon as the workers in the parable of the Vineyard Laborers open their mouths (Mt 20:1–16) we learn something about them.

INTERPRETIVE MODEL

Via, 152

> The flaw in the grumbling workers which comes to expression in the recognition scene (20:12) is more serious than an envy which cannot tolerate kindness shown to others.... The fact that they insisted on the application of a merit system—reward should be exactly proportionate to achievement—shows that they believed themselves capable of maintaining their position in the world, of deserving their reward. If someone, however, is rewarded, not on the basis of his own achievement, but on the basis of another's generosity, then there is an incalculable element in human relationships, and the sense of being able to provide one's own security is seriously challenged. In the face of this challenge the grumbling workers still insisted on a merit order. Their desire to have their security within their own grasp caused them to see the incalculable, not as graciousness, but as injustice. Rather than seeing themselves as self-centered they accused the householder of unfairness.

In the workers' *talk* Via can hear their *emotion* (indignation), in the emotion he sees their *motives* ("envy" and the wish "to have their security within their own grasp"), and in the motives he reads their *attitude:* that they deserved their reward. (Here the image mirrors the perils of overestimating the merit of having "left everything to follow"—19:27.) Finally their attitude shows their character as self-centered. Emotion, motive, and attitude are things to look for when studying characters' talk to find their traits. Donahue uses the same method (107–8) to gain important insights on the one-talent man in the Talents (Mt 25:14–30; cf. Lk 19:11–27).

Exercise on the Tenants (Mt 21:33–46)

According to Gundry (427) "'Heir' indicates that the tenant farmers thought the owner had died and the son was coming to claim the vineyard as his inheritance. In killing him, they thought they would avoid a legal battle in court and gain the vineyard for themselves by right of possession." Assume that this is correct. Identify the emotions, motives, and attitudes expressed in (a) the owner's speech ("They will respect my son") and (b) the tenants' speech ("This is the heir; come, let us kill him and have his inheritance"). How well does each speech correspond with reality? To answer, complete the following.

> God's sending Jesus : Jewish leaders = the owner's sending
>   his son : the tenants
> with respect to _____
>
> Jewish leaders : Israel = the tenants : the vineyard
> with respect to _____

In characterization, as in other things, we know that actions speak even louder than words—in the Lost Son (Lk 15:11–32), for example.

INTERPRETIVE MODEL

Bailey, 1976, 193

> True to his character, the older son is initially suspicious. A son with a normal relationship with his family would enter immediately, eager to join the joy, whatever its source. On hearing the beat of the music he knows immediately that it is a joyous occasion. Village rhythms are specific and known. The older son does not rush in as expected. He is unnaturally suspicious.

Bailey infers that the older son's *attitude* in hanging back is one of suspicion. The reasonable assumptions are that his *motive* is to avoid undesirable entanglements (he lacks "a normal relationship with his family"), and that his *emotion* is fear (in addition to the anger specified in v 28). So too the Pharisees (Lk 15:1–2), who have yet to learn that all this affects their relationship not just with people but with God.

> elder son : father and younger son = Pharisees : God and "sinners"
> with respect to fear, aloofness, and suspicion

As characters' words need to be measured against reality, so too their actions. Part of the unjust judge's situation (Lk 18:1–8) is his occupation and its demands. By contrasting his impious *way* of life with his *place* in life, Scott (178–79) fully justifies calling him shameless. Such discrepancies between action and reality can have various kinds of meaning; compare the vinedresser's plea for the fig tree (Lk 13:8) in the face of its apparently hopeless barrenness, and the father's welcome of the prodigal without any test of his deserving (Lk 15:20–24).

EXERCISE

Exercises on the Two Builders (Mt 7:24–27) and the Lost Son (Lk 15:11–32)

1. In so many words Jesus characterizes the second builder as "a foolish man." Still we can nuance the character, and Jesus' theme, by applying this interpretive question: How do the man's actions ignore reality?

    > some of Jesus' hearers : the opportunity of his message =
    >   the foolish builder : his building
    > with respect to _____

    (Cf. the Tower Builder and the Warring King, Lk 14:26–33.)

2. The elder son characterizes his brother as a profligate and nothing more (v 30). Thus his protest reflects bafflement at his father's treatment of the younger son, which implies some quite different assessment, and to him seems out of touch with reality. What do the father's actions say about the prodigal, and, by analogy, about God's view of sinners?

_____

See also Kilgallen (1993, 50–57) on the Empty House (Lk 11:24–26).

CHOICE AND CHANGE

Human nature in an individual is never altogether fixed. For better or worse it changes gradually, as a person chooses how to respond to change. Often in stories—less often, perhaps in real life—some crisis sparks a dramatic change, at least in attitude and motives. Most of Jesus' stories are too short and his characters too sketchy for much character development. There are, however, a few cases of dramatic change—some sad, such as the unmerciful servant's (Mt 18:23–35), where the wrong choice wastes a golden opportunity for growth.

INTERPRETIVE MODEL

Donahue, 76–78

> [The first servant's plea for himself] is in the order of justice; the king operates in the order of mercy out of compassion.
>
> The second act plays out the result of the servant's faulty understanding. When he goes out and hears the request of the second servant, he hears an echo of his own disposition. He enters again the familiar world of strict justice. The forgiveness and mercy that he

received were something that simply happened to him, not something that changes his way of viewing the world. His self-understanding remains unaltered by the gift he received. The statement of the "lord" in v. 33 is the moment of tragic revelation of why he acted as he did, "Should not you have had mercy on your fellow servant, as I had mercy on you?" The master says, in effect: Even given your predisposition to view the world through the eyes of strict justice, you should have seen that the mercy which was "right" in your case was also owed to your fellow servant. Paradoxically, then, mercy becomes justice and justice or "the right order" between God and humanity is maintained through mercy. The Matthean addition of v. 35 stresses that forgiveness must be "from your heart." This is a warning that unless the gospel transforms the innermost dispositions of its hearers, they will act in much the same fashion as the first servant. The Jewish-Christian letter [of] James, with its accustomed directness, conveys a similar view: "For judgment is without mercy to one who has shown no mercy; yet mercy triumphs over judgment" (James 2:13). The parable thus conveys the precondition for a proper Christian ethic, and not simply an exhortation to forgiveness.

We may feel simple horror or satisfaction at the punishment; that is a response to *plot*. If so, we need to respond to *character* too. Jesus' challenge goes beyond demanding purely symptomatic *acts* of forgiveness; he wants a change of heart, which the servant fails to attain.

What of persons who seize their special opportunity? The five- and ten-talent men (Mt 25:14–30), the good Samaritan (Lk 10:25–37), the unjust steward (Lk 16:1–3) are good examples, though none is given enough prior history for us to trace the kind

of change that we call character development. It is otherwise with
the prodigal.

EXERCISE

Exercise on the Lost Son (Lk 15:11–32)

The moment when the prodigal "came to his senses" (v 17) is
one of the most dramatic changes to be found among Jesus' para-
ble-characters. The story ends with another equally weighty
moment of choice, this time the elder son's. Describe how the
younger son's choice alters his inner being attitudes, as well as his
motives and actions—thereby illuminating what Jesus says about
tax collectors and other sinners. Describe the elder son's opportunity (vv 31–32) to change—thereby illuminating what Jesus says
to the Pharisees.

See also Sellew (239–53) on the significance of choices in
parables of Luke's gospel.

RELATIONSHIPS

A particular relationship between characters may be important either as a subject of interpretation or as a tool to assist it. We
use relationships as interpretive tools when we study Jesus' *character foils*—persons juxtaposed so that the traits of one highlight the
character of the other, and sometimes vice versa. For example, Via's
discussion (170–72) of relationships in the Lost Son (Lk 15:11–
32) reveals that two brothers who seem entirely unlike have, in
fact, more than one ironically striking similarity. Both are "in the
wrong place"; and consequently the father must "go out" to both.
Both sons need and receive the father's grace; this is another irony
of Jesus' response to the Pharisees' complacent criticism.

In analyzing motives and the effects of character foils we can
profit greatly by Breech's comments on the Vineyard Laborers (Mt
20:1–16).

INTERPRETIVE MODEL

Breech, 153

> The labourers are suffering from value delusion, meaning that they quite unconsciously establish the value of things and persons only in terms that allow them to feel good about themselves. . . . They blame [the householder] because they feel right and feel that he has done something that contradicts their mode of valuation. *His* mode of evaluating his own behaviour, as we have seen, proceeds by examining the concrete bonds that he has established with the various groups of workers, and the concrete bond that he has with his own vineyard. . . . He concludes that he has done them no wrong. And yet they grumble. Why? . . . They raise the principle of equal pay for equal work because they think of money as a symbol which establishes the relative value of people, and understand themselves and their own value in terms of what they earn in comparison with what others earn. . . . They want everything to be controlled by a system that prevents anyone from benefiting unexpectedly from someone else's spontaneous gift.

Here are shrewd questions about owner and workers alike. Their speech reveals the contrasting perspectives on life which breed the conflict. The contrast conveys Jesus' point about how high God's thoughts are above human legalism.

> workers' attitude : owner's attitude = human thoughts : God's thoughts
> with respect to the contrast of legalism and freedom

Human relationships reward other kinds of special consideration, as in Breech's remarks (26–28) on the Children in the Marketplace

(Mt 11:16–19; Lk 7:31–35). His analysis of *group dynamics* suits this parable because Jesus pursues his conflict with the Pharisees by addressing their group dynamics.

Exercise on the Sabbath Mishap (Lk 14:1–6), the Places at Table (vv 7–14), and the Great Supper (vv 15–24)

The conflict with the Pharisees continues through most of this chapter in three analogies, and through the next chapter's Lost Sheep, Coin, and Son. How does Jesus' advice give the function of character foils to the competitive guests (v 7) and Jesus' host (v 12)? How does the Great Supper make the originally invited guests (vv 18–20) into foils of those who actually take part in the feast (vv 21–23)? What are the implications for the point(s) Jesus is making on this occasion? How does Jesus use all three of these analogies to address the group dynamics of his Sabbath meal at the Pharisee's house?

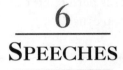

6

SPEECHES

The characters' actual words dominate the Unjust Steward (Lk 16:1–13), and the story comes close enough to the form of a stage-play to read like *dramatic narrative*. But usually a parable paraphrases or summarizes what characters say. This *indirect speech* sets off the occasional *direct speech* with a special emphasis, as in the elder brother's moment of discovery in the Lost Son (Lk 15:26–27): "So he called one of the servants and asked him what was going on. 'Your brother has come,' he replied."

SOLILOQUY

When a solitary character like the rich fool (Lk 12:13–21) thinks out loud—in a *soliloquy* that "excludes others from his story" (Scott, 133)—we are apt to learn more than usual from his words.

INTERPRETIVE MODEL

Scott, 135, 139

> The man addresses himself formally as "Self." . . . The text does not say, ". . . and he said to himself, 'Self,'" but ". . . and I will say to my self, 'Self.'" The rich man usurps the narrator's control of the story. . . .
>
> The literary technique of the parable, with the disappearing narrator, replicates the rich man's taking over

the story. His idolatry, his usurpation of story and harvest, and his crowding out all around him can only be
remedied by God's intervention. All other characters
have been eliminated.

Scott notes a cluster of *unconscious ironies* (cf. part 2.3), features of the fool's speech that become ironic in the light of God's
reply. First, with his four *I will*'s (cf. Jas 4:13–16) he speaks as if
his decisions determined his destiny; but God will do that. Second, he presumes to hoard his wealth; but God says, "Whose shall
these things be?" (KJV). Third, he expects "many years" of the good
life; but God says "This very night. . . ." Fourth, he really thinks he
is soliloquizing—that he has shut out everyone else; but the voice
of God, who hears his thoughts, comes to him out of nowhere.
This most dramatic irony helps explain why the conclusion so
strongly affects one's imagination. All the ironies help justify God's
characterization: "You fool!"

Other characters' talk unwittingly creates similar ironies. In
his recognition speech the prodigal devises a face-saving proposi-
tion—"Make me like one of your hired men" (Lk 15:19)—to be
preempted by his father's precipitous welcome. The unjust judge's
"Even though I don't fear God or care about men" (Lk 18:4) makes
his faults so obvious one wonders how he can hear himself and still
miss them. And the tenants' culminating crime makes the owner's
"They will respect my son" (Mk 12:6) tragically ironic.

One soliloquizer not overtaken by unconscious ironies is the
unjust steward; his accuracy about his present and future (Lk 16:4)
befits his celebrated shrewdness. But here is a different function.
Set off from the surrounding dialogue, his soliloquy is the dramatic
marker of a crisis of choice and the steward's momentous question
(v 3), "What shall I do now?" which dramatizes the urgency of
Jesus' message to his disciples.

people of this world : their own kind > people of light :
   their own kind
with respect to shrewdness (v 8)

worldly treasure : worldly people < true riches : disciples
with respect to trustworthiness required

So too the rich fool with his "What shall I do?" and the prodi-gal son, and the unjust judge: "The change comes, as it frequently does in the parables, when the narrative moves to dialogue, in this case a soliloquy ('he said to himself')" (Donahue 183).

EXERCISE

Exercise on the Pharisee and Publican (Lk 18:9–14)

Jesus calls the Pharisee's prayer a soliloquy (v 11; cf. Mk 12:40); it too is a moment of choice tragically unrecognized. Describe its unconscious ironies and their significance for Jesus' intended meaning(s).

DIALOGUE

Like soliloquy, dialogue can accent a characterization or a cri-sis—both, when the tenants say: "This is the heir. Come, let's kill him, and the inheritance will be ours" (Mk 12:7), a quasi-solilo-quy of conspiracy. In the Great Supper (Lk 14:15–24) the dialogue marks the episodes.

INTERPRETIVE MODEL

Bailey, 1980, 92–93

After the introduction the dramatic action ... divides into seven speeches. We could even call the parable "The Banquet of the Seven Speeches." These seven fall naturally into seven stanzas (almost seven scenes) with certain key ideas repeating in the first four and then other key ideas repeating in the last three. The master gives three speeches. Each of them begins with a command related to the gathering of the guests. There are two invitations to the original guests at the beginning of the parable, and two invitations to outsiders (although to different people) at the end.

First Bailey uses the speeches simply to identify the episodes. Comparing them leads him next to insights of plot analysis: the parallel commands, the paired invitations at the beginning (vv 16–17) and the end (vv 21, 23). Do these structural features help us find Jesus' meaning? That is the final step.

Exercise on the Unmerciful Servant (Mt 18:23–35)

Study the alternation of narrative and dialogue in this parable to discover its major episodes. Write a proportional analogy to convey Jesus' main point in each episode. Is one of these three points *the* main point? Why?

Donahue's commentary (153–57) on the Lost Son (Lk 15:11–32) shows how to connect various interpretive considerations with dialogue. He links the dialogue with no less than eleven other literary features that we have surveyed in part 2. (1) He notes that the dialogue points us to the characters' *relationships* and all that they entail. (2) He reads in the recognition speech the prodigal's *emotion* (fear), *motive* (desire for relief), and *attitude* (contrition). (3) In the soliloquy he finds a key to interpretation—the son's sin of apostasy. (Cf. Lk 15:1–2, and the Pharisees' belief that Jewish "sinners" were not true Israelites at all.) (4) He sees the *self-characterizing* quality of the son's speech: "I am no longer worthy." (5) He remarks on the rhetorical force of a *repetition* that stimulates the imagination about narrative details: "Rehearsing it as he makes his way back" (155). (6) He links this repeated speech with "one of the major motifs of the parable"—the son's full, even unprecedented, restoration. (7) He notes the effect of *verbal irony:* "He is not allowed to finish his prepared speech" (155), and *irony of situation:* "He is . . . raised to a position greater than when he left" (156). (8) He makes a point of the *connotations* of the elder son's speech to his father. (9) He describes the rhetorical *balance* of the elder son's triple complaint and the younger son's triple confession. (10) He draws out the significance of the brothers as character *foils,* with special reference to the connotations of the elder son's speech ("this son of yours"). (11) He reads the father's attitude, motive, and emotion in both the *denotation* of his speech ("everything I have is yours") and its connotations ("son" and "your brother"). And he addresses many literary topics with little of their distracting technical terminology.

EXERCISE

Exercise on the Barren Fig Tree (Lk 13:6–9)

Even this simplest of dialogues—two speeches—has its implications. Find as many as you can, considering diction (part 2.1), rhetoric (2.2), narrative climax (2.4), personal crisis (2.4), and various other aspects of character (2.5). How do all these things add up to Jesus' intended meaning(s)?

7
SETTING

The physical and social situation of the characters should be considered along with plot, character, and speeches. *Setting* in this sense is quite a different thing from what we call a parable's *Sitz im Leben*—the context or "setting" described in the evangelist's narrative as including the locale, audience, and occasion of the parable's telling. As Scott notes (178) in the Unjust Judge (Lk 18:1–8), setting may contribute to characterization in the man's "initial marks of honor"; "he is a judge, and he belongs to an urban elite."

The Pharisee and Publican (Lk 18:9–14) has a symbolic setting.

INTERPRETIVE MODEL

Scott, 94

> The parable begins with two men going up to the temple to pray, and it concludes with the same two men going down to their respective houses. The motion to temple and back to house constitutes an inclusio that rounds off the parable. The symbolic distance between secular space (home) and sacred space (temple) replicates the distance between characters, but more fundamentally . . . the temple conjures up a religious standard that gives value to both the characters. The Pharisee is good and the tax collector bad, because of the religious standard represented by the temple. If they had gone to a Roman law court, their values and the parable's point

of view would have been different. Even more, the temple could not exist without Pharisees (insiders) and tax collectors (outsiders). The temple is the map, the metaphor, that stands for the insiders and outsiders. Since this is a parable of contrast, the temple will map out the contrast. The contrast form does not decide in advance whether the first or second one will be favored, although the temple map surely favors the Pharisee.

Scott has asked fruitful questions in order to describe the situation as he does. What motion is there between the two specified locales (temple and house)? What does the "distance" (distinction) between these "spaces" signify? What particular human value is attached to the main setting (the temple)? How does this affect characterization (of the two principals)? To which character does this direct our sympathies?

EXERCISE

Exercises on the Good Samaritan (Lk 10:25–37), the Lost Son (Lk 15:11–32), and the Great Supper (Lk 14:15–24)

1. It might be useful to apply Scott's questions to the Good Samaritan and the Lost Son. No list of questions, however, will do for every case. Scott's creative task is to find the questions that suit his parable. Another parable demands other questions; in the Rich Man and Lazarus one should ask how the next world functions as a foil for this. Devise and answer special questions about the settings of the Good Samaritan and the Lost Son. Which question(s) do you judge most significant for Jesus' purposes in the parable, as depicted in Luke's context?

2. Scott notes that the temple creates social groups—the insiders and outsiders. Devise this sort of question for the Great Supper and then answer it.

8
POINT OF VIEW

There are two sides to every story, as we say, because people's perceptions are as different as their diverse attitudes, beliefs, and preoccupations. We call your side of a story (or your opinion about it) your "point of view" because you interpret an event by your perception of it; you "view" it from a mental "vantage *point*" peculiar to your gender, age, experience, religion, politics, etc. Narrative *point of view*—understood as still another feature of story to be interpreted—denotes the psychological perspective of the person(s) through whose eyes we see what happens in a story, and by which we may be inclined toward a particular opinion or judgment about it.

DOMINANT PERSPECTIVE

The point of view in the Tenants (Mk 12:1–12) has been variously identified.

INTERPRETIVE MODEL

Via, 134–35

It is claimed by Baird that the figure of the owner dominates the story, while Michaelis seems to be most interested in the question of his son. From the standpoint of the story itself both of these approaches are

> somewhat eccentric in view of the fact that the formal shape of the story derives from the experience of the wicked tenants. The beginning relates that a man let out his vineyard to tenants and went away. In the middle part we see what happened when he attempted to collect the proceeds which were rightfully due to him, and we have the hint of an insight into why the tenants behaved as they did. The ending tells about—or at least suggests—the destruction which will come to the tenants as a result of their behavior.

We see through the eyes of the protagonist first, as he plants, sets, digs, builds, lets out his vineyard, goes away, and sends a servant back (12:1–2). But the tenant-antagonists dominate the rest of the action. Probably the hearer's perspective will shift from the vineyard owner to become aligned either with the teller's distanced point of view or with the perspective of the tenants. This creates interesting tensions: for us readers of Mark, because we do not approve their actions or share their way of thinking; and for the Jewish leaders, because they would resist Jesus' pointed identification.

One determinant of narrative point of view, then, is plain physical dominance of the scene. Another has to do with end stress; the outcome of the story is the tenants' outcome. The language used to designate characters can influence our perspective as well (e.g., Scott [122] on the Lost Son): "The parable began with two sons (*hyios*), one identified as younger (*neōteros*) and the other, later, as elder (*presybyteros*), and the narrator maintains the father's perspective by referring to sons."

SYMPATHETIC IDENTIFICATION

Identifying the narrative point of view can help us define the hearer's sympathies in the Good Samaritan (Lk 10:25–37).

INTERPRETIVE MODEL

Funk, 212

> From what perspective is the parable told? Initially at least, the account compels the hearer to put himself in the place of that nameless fellow jogging along the wild and dangerous road. Straightway he finds himself the object of a murderous attack which leaves him stripped, beaten, and half-dead. While lying helpless in the ditch, he is aware that the priest and Levite pass by with only an apprehensive glance. It does not matter to him whether their callousness can be excused or justified, and if the hearer (as victim) is a layman, his secret anticlericalism is confirmed. The priest or Levite as hearer will, of course, be incensed. At this juncture the lay hearer will anticipate the arrival of a benign layman on the scene; the ecclesiastical listener, muttering under his breath, will expect no less. In the teeth of just such anticipations, to the utter amazement and chagrin of every listener as Jew (the previous dichotomy is bridged in an instant), a hated enemy, a half-breed, a perverter of true religion comes into view and ministers to the helpless victim when he is powerless to prevent him. While still in inner turmoil over this unexpected turn of events, the hearer is brought up short with the question: "Which of these three, do you think, proved neighbor ... ?" It is a question on which the Jew chokes. The lawyer in the Lucan account cannot bring himself to pronounce the name of that hated "neighbor," but he can hardly avoid the answer which the parable demands.

Funk implies two sufficient reasons why the audience will identify with the man in the ditch: the victim dominates the scene, while others come and go; and since the crisis of the story is the victim's, so will be the outcome.

But there is a third reason. Inevitably an audience adopts some point of view, ordinarily inclining to a *sympathetic character*, i.e., one with whom they can easily identify. Scott (198–200) uses the process of elimination: because a Jewish lay audience will not identify with priest, Levite, or Samaritan, he rightly finds the hearer in the dilemma of unwillingly identifying with the man in the ditch in his dependence on the hated Samaritan, or else having to attempt to reject a very compelling story. The victim might well refuse a Samaritan's help if he could. Despite his bias, however, his point of view is definitive for the story; he cannot ignore the Samaritan's help even if he "cannot believe it."

In the Lost Son (Lk 15:11–32), on the other hand, we adopt the point of view of a character whose perspective is far too limited to be definitive (Via, 169): "The prodigal . . . is incapable of knowing what possibilities for good might come to him until they do come." Eventually his point of view is eclipsed by the father's greater scope of perspective, as demonstrated by his separate efforts to restore both sons to family harmony. But among the pigs and pods the younger son sees things in a way that we must share, if we are to understand the tax collectors and sinners (Lk 15:1–2) as Jesus does.

Scott's exemplary approach (274–78) to the Unmerciful Servant (Mt 18:23–35) asks of each episode: Which character's point of view does the audience adopt? He points initially to the narrator rather than either the king or the servant, because both of the latter are too fantastic, and the king is too evil. The Jewish hearer's natural responses, as he notes, are fascination with the fantastic and moral superiority. Once the other servants appear, Scott's leading question gets a new answer: first in the servants' indignation and then in the king's judgment the hearer simply recognizes the point of view already established (of moral superiority, if not of distance from the fantastic). It is not the hearer who has shifted ground but the characters and the situation. Though slavery of the first servant and his family was an intolerable judgment for the debt alone, imprisonment with torture might well seem to a Jewish hearer like a punishment that fits the crime of the servant's harshness with his fellow servant.

Here is a very significant fact, commonly acknowledged about many parables because it is indispensable to understanding. The story's point of view makes the hearer participate directly in a judgment independent of the characters', and subsequent events ratify it. Point of view may be more than a window for the audience's passive observation; it may pull the hearer into active involvement.

EXERCISE

Exercises on the Talents (Mt 25:14–30) and the Unjust Judge (Lk 18:1–9)

1. For the Talents use Scott's method of tracing the point of view through the story, describing its significance for the audience's responses. Include the following questions, and devise more. With which person(s)—including the narrator—is the point of view primarily associated? What are the cues? What does the location of the point of view, as well as any shifts in it, contribute to the plot, the characterization, the emotions, and the ideas of the parable?

2. The Unjust Judge is sometimes called "the Persistent Widow" with the implication that it is "her story." Whose point of view does the audience adopt? Whose perspective is more expansive, the judge's or the widow's? What other considerations seem important? What effect does the story's point of view (as you define it) have on the audience's *ideas* and *emotions?*

While telling a full-fledged story, Jesus is often a "self-effac-ing" narrator, unlike story tellers who by hints or outright state-ment interpret as they go. Usually Jesus' editorializing comes in introductions and conclusions, as suits the natural separation of vehicle and tenor in analogy.

9
TONE

Rarely is human language entirely cold-blooded. Even mathematicians can get excited enough to call a proof elegant. For this reason we will not find the meaning of a parable solely in rational thought. Just because of our humanity, the whole meaning combines mutually dependent ideas and feelings. We can call a parable an analogy and express its meaning in proportional statements without ignoring its emotional content. In every section of part 2 interpreters grapple with the feelings that the parables inspire— i.e., their *tone*—as well as the ideas. Many of our terms for various features of narrative denote emotional effects: the "connotations" and "sensory effects" of words, rhetorical effects such as "irony," the "suspense," "climax," and "surprise" of a plot, "sympathetic" and "unsympathetic" characters, the "atmosphere" of a setting.

We should consider how emotion and reason work together in a parable's meaning, and how the parable moves our feelings in the first place. It helps to note how *theme* (idea) determines *tone* in a parable while tone is simultaneously shaping theme. In his interpretation of the Unmerciful Servant (Mt 18:23–35) Donahue (74– 76) presents ideas and feelings precisely as we find them when we read a parable—distinct but inseparable—and throughout he keeps describing their interaction. At the same time he accounts for the source of the various emotions, both the characters' and the hearers'. (His three "acts" are Mt 18:23–27, 28–30, 31–34, with 35 as a "Matthean epilogue.")

163

How does the parable generate feelings? Donahue points first to the *actions* that create the characters' bad and good fortune, and then to the audience's resulting emotional involvement to which he rightly attributes the force of the parable. The king's first action, sentencing a servant with his family to enslavement, must make the poor man feel terrible, and the audience too: "An unpayable debt to a heartless master is pitiable" (75). Even the king is affected; he remits the sentence because he "took pity on him" (v 27). Now the king's generosity inspires surprise, even shock. We feel happiness as well, and so must the servant, though *his* actions immediately create a sudden alteration. Seeing his own debtor makes him furious and implacable, as we gather when he chokes him and puts him in prison. Now other servants are greatly "distressed" (v 31) and so are we. And so it goes; actions bring good or ill fortune, with answerable emotions in characters and audience.

Donahue makes another important point about the *progression* of the action: from ill fortune to good to ill again, in the case of the first servant. This complication heightens the audience's emotional involvement. Such ups and downs are what make a plot work upon an audience; the more, the better.

Donahue shows how the *ordering* of the plot creates suspense about "the reason for this threatening situation" (74–75). He also points to the evocative *language* of the parable in describing debt, mercy, and the characters' powerful feelings. Moreover he implies that shifting to *direct speech* can emphasize the feelings of a moment—e.g., "Have patience. . . ." And *characterization* contributes to the audience's feeling as well; when the forgiven servant refuses to forgive, "The person with whom we rejoiced earlier now becomes repulsive" (76). One more source of feeling is *irony of situation*: "In v. 34 there is a tragic irony for the first servant in that now he will have what he originally requested, time to pay his debt, only the time will be spent in prison" (76).

How do thought and feeling combine in the parable? While tracking the audience's sympathies from one character to another throughout, Donahue at the same time is describing how thought directs feeling, and vice versa. Why does he say that the first servant attracts our sympathies in Act I? Because the action gives the audience *ideas:* the debt is impossible, and the master is implacable; therefore the servant deserves our pity. Once we start to pity him, ideas have prompted *feelings.* Similarly, our first idea about this king (that such a tyrant would not show pity) sets us up for the shock to our feelings when he remits the entire debt. In Act II Donahue identifies several ideas that are prompted by the first servant's treatment of the second. The most important of these are the disparity in the amounts owing and the first servant's greater heartlessness than his master's, because together they create the paradox that prompts the crucial shift of our sympathies away from him.

Thus far ideas have been prompting feelings, but in Act III (at least) feelings prompt our ideas when our indignation leads us to judge the first servant just as his fellow servants do: he deserves to be punished. In the end, is our response to the outcome primarily rational or emotional? On Donahue's assessment of the tragic irony of verse 34, one could go either way.

We are acculturated to think of "meaning" primarily, or even entirely, as rational content, but we should be equally sensitive to tone. In other parables the effects of tone have all the diversity and interest of Jesus' various plots, characters, and themes. See, for examples, Scott (171) on the Great Supper (Lk 14:15–24), Stein (126–28) on the Vineyard Laborers (Mt 20:1–16), and Donahue (55) on the Tenants (Mt 21:33–45; Mk 12:1–12; Lk 20:9–19).

EXERCISE

Exercise on the Rich Man and Lazarus (Lk 16:19–31)

Think of the first eight topics in part 2 as features that contribute to tone. Study each one as a cue to the emotions of characters and audience in this parable, and distinguish as many points as you can. Organize them into a play-by-play description of the characters' thoughts and feelings as they prompt each other, and of the audience's thoughts and feelings as they prompt each other, including any shifts in the audience's sympathies. Write a summary statement of the meaning of the parable, taking equal account of theme and tone.

Part 2 catalogs the parables' internal features: verbal (chapter 1), rhetorical (2–3), and narrative (4–8). Adding up the effects of all these features gives us a method of mapping any audience's response, from the "ideal hearer" who knows, hears, and responds perfectly, to the most stupid or stubborn of Jesus' actual hearers. While the latter is not irrelevant to understanding, the former is crucial. Describing the ideal hearer's response puts us well on the way to articulating the meaning of a parable. Other models of this audience-response criticism are Funk and Scott on the Good Samaritan. Each takes account of a wide variety of the parables' verbal, rhetorical, and narrative components.

When we evaluate the significance of any of the intrinsic features surveyed in part 2, our judgment should be directed in part by features external to the parables but no less essential to interpretation. To these we now turn.

SUMMARY OF PART 2

1. Any internal feature of a parable may be crucial to its meaning, especially as a cue to the extent and limits of the allegorical symbolism.
2. The *diction* of the text may have special significance of denotation, connotation, or sensory effect; so may the *grammatical and rhetorical structures*.

3. Both in the image of a parable and in its context, *irony* may include paradox, overstatement, understatement, and inapposite answers—all requiring special alertness in the interpreter.

4. The *plot* of a parable may reveal Jesus' intent in his handling of the elements of the story: their selection, climactic effect, arrangement in comic and tragic sequences, and proportions.

5. In such simple stories, any evident trait of a participant's *character* is apt to contribute to the parable's meaning, especially in crises of choice and change, and in relationships.

6. *Direct speech*, in either soliloquy or dialogue, usually highlights facts of special importance to interpretation.

7. The physical and social *setting* of a story typically helps to focus the significance of the plot, characters, and speeches.

8. The perspective created by Jesus' choice of a narrative *point of view* is one of his means of directing our response to a story, especially our sympathies for the characters.

9. The *tone* of a parable, determined by the features already mentioned, may indicate conclusively what we should make of the ideas that the parable evokes.

PART
III

External Features
of the Parables

No hearer can approach a parable without many preunderstandings. The extrinsic features of a parable are the mental equipment that an audience brings to a hearing. As Gerhardsson says (335), it is not sound exegesis to cut Jesus' stories "out of their frames in the Gospels and treat them as wild texts designed to function as naked narratives with indeterminable messages." Many interpretations in part 2 have invoked some special feature of ancient Middle-Eastern culture or some aspect of the parables' literary context in the Gospels. Many more cultural assumptions and theological affinities have been taken for granted. Such externals are our focus in part 3.

1

ACCULTURATION

Cultural conditioning affects our response to what we hear and read just as much as our response to anything else. In some respects we are very conscious of the differences between the culture of Jesus' time and our own, and sometimes we can easily compensate. Many significant features of his culture, however, are much more foreign to us than we can guess without intensive study. We may confidently misinterpret a parable simply because we are too ignorant of life in ancient Palestine, or of Jewish theology, history, folklore, and symbols. The more we know about the acculturation of Jesus' audience in all these respects, the more sure we can be about our interpretation.

PALESTINIAN LIFE

"All the Jews do not eat unless they give their hands a ceremonial washing," says Mark (7:3) in his thoughtfulness for non-Jewish readers. We know that Jesus' culture is not our own; the parables dramatize the difference. As with all cross-cultural studies, scholars' extensive research both reassures and troubles: we understand many things better than we used to, but as discoveries accumulate we wonder how much of our ignorance is yet to be exposed and how serious it is. We must learn what we can, such as these facts about the Lost Son (Lk 15:11–32).

INTERPRETIVE MODEL

Bailey, 1976, 176–77, 183

> The key to understanding the prodigal's intentions in regard to his father is found in his face-saving plan. . . . As a "hired servant" he will be a free man with his own income living independently in the local village. His social status will not be inferior to that of his father and his brother. He can maintain his pride and his independence. But there is more.
>
> If the prodigal becomes a hired servant, he may be able to pay back what he has lost. . . . In short, he will save himself. He wants no grace. . . . Sonship has certain distinct disadvantages. If he accepts sonship, he will have to live with his brother and be fed from his brother's property. He will again be under the total authority of his father. He will be denied the self-satisfaction of having "earned his own way."

A modern reader would hardly guess that becoming a hired servant was face-saving; nor could we recognize the son's acceptance of sonship as repentance.

father : son = God : *repentant* tax collectors and sinners
with respect to joy in recovery

Similarly, when Jesus addresses the parable of the Barren Fig Tree (Lk 13:6–9) to the crowd (12:54), we may sense the main thrust but not feel its edge for lack of some key information (Scott, 336). "The owner has been coming for three years. Normally fig trees bear annually, usually from early spring until late fall. Three years was the normal time for maturation of a fig tree. . . . The passage of three years indicates that the fig tree is hopelessly infertile."

Why *should* it continue to waste the ground? And why should the vinedresser continue to invest his time? His hope is a dramatic

symbol of God's longsuffering mercy with a stiff-necked generation for whom the image clearly implies little or no hope.

crowd : extended opportunity = fig tree: year's reprieve
with respect to small likelihood of change

When we read between the lines, unconsciously inferring
Jesus' culture from the parables, we tend to assume that what we
see is typical—for example, that women regularly baked three
measures' worth of bread at once, or that imprisonment for debt
was a Jewish custom. Thus we need certain facts in order to distinguish the commonplace from the unusual in the Leaven (Mt
13:33), and Jewish culture from foreign culture in Going to Court
(Mt 5:25–26).

INTERPRETIVE MODEL

Gundry, 268, 87

> Three measures of flour amounted to about a bushel,
> give or take a little, and made the largest amount of
> dough a woman could knead. The bread would feed a
> crowd of about one hundred—enough for a festive
> occasion, as in Gen 18:6, where Sarah made bread from
> three measures of flour for the Lord and two of his
> angels. Is Jesus hinting at the messianic banquet?
>
> In a Jewish setting, reference to the Gentiles' cruel
> practice of throwing debtors in prison, where they had
> no way of earning money to pay their debts, was sure to
> grab attention and put a warning stress on the judg-
> ment portrayed.

Cultural information can tell us which details are symbolic.
We may thus avoid overreading: Bailey warns (1976, 124 n.25)
that in the Friend at Midnight (Lk 11:5–8) the lack of repayment
can hardly function as part of Jesus' tenor, since it is not a culturally
significant feature of the vehicle. Or we may discover more of

Jesus' theme: e.g., stripping the victim in the Good Samaritan (Lk 10:25–37) is more than realistic detail.

INTERPRETIVE MODELS

Donahue, 133; Bailey, 1980, 42–43

According to the law of the time, a person with an unpaid debt could be enslaved until the debt was paid (cf. Matt. 18:23–35). Since the injured man was robbed and stripped—deprived of all resources—he could have been at the mercy of the innkeeper, a profession that had a bad reputation in antiquity for dishonesty and violence. The Samaritan assures the injured man's freedom and independence. The parable here addresses its subsequent use in Christian ethics. It is not enough simply to enter the world of the neighbor with care and compassion; one must enter and leave it in such a way that the neighbor is given freedom along with the very help that is offered. (Donahue)

The wounded traveler's condition is not a curious incidental. . . . Tomb paintings demonstrate conclusively that Jewish and non-Jewish costumes could be distinguished by sight in Palestine in the first century. . . . But what if the man beside the road was stripped? He was thereby reduced to a mere human being in need. He belonged to no man's ethnic or religious community! It is such a person that the robbers leave wounded beside the road. Who will turn aside to render aid? (Bailey)

EXERCISE

Exercise on the Lost Son (Lk 15:11–32), the Talents (Mt 25:14–30), and the Great Supper (Lk 14:15–24)

Bailey (1980, 132–33) introduces the social value of shame to explain the Unjust Judge (Lk 18:1–8) and the Tenants (Lk 20:9–

19). Construct proportions to show how this information illuminates the character, motives, and actions of the elder son, the one-
talent man, the originally-invited guests.

> One of the sharpest criticisms possible of an adult in the Mid-
> dle Eastern village today is *mā jikhtashǐ* ("he does not feel
> shame")....
>
> The problem with this judge is ... his inability to sense
> the evil of his actions in the presence of one who should make
> him ashamed.... We have precisely the same concept and the
> same word in the parable of the Rebellious Tenants in Luke
> 20:13. The tenants ... treat the servants of the owner shame-
> fully. Finally the master says, "I will send my beloved son; it
> may be they will feel shame before (*entrapēsontai*) him (so
> translated in all Syriac and Arabic versions). The hope is not
> that they might treat him kindly, but rather that in his pres-
> ence they might feel ashamed of what they have done and give
> up their rebellious acts. But there also the tenants involved
> *could not be shamed.* In both texts the Greek word carries this
> meaning. Middle Eastern culture requires it and Middle East-
> ern fathers give us this meaning in their translations. Thus we
> have in Luke 18 a clear picture of a *very* difficult man. He has
> no fear of God; the cry of "for God's sake" will do no good.

For a wealth of further information about how life in Palestine bears on the parables, see Bailey (1976, 1980), Derrett, and
Scott.

JEWISH THEOLOGY

The religious beliefs of Jesus' hearers affected their responses to
his parables. If we ignore their beliefs we may mistake the response
that he expects. Sometimes the text explains them (e.g., Mk 7:2–4;
Lk 7:39; 15:1–2), but often not. Thus the context of the Wolves in
Sheep's Clothing (Mt 7:15) needs a doctrinal explanation.

INTERPRETIVE MODEL

Beare, 196–97

> There was a generally accepted belief in contemporary
> Judaism that prophecy had long ceased. All revelation
> was given in the Law.... Once Judaism developed into
> a religion of the Book any new "prophet" was bound to
> be regarded with suspicion. In such a community, there
> was no need for a warning against "false prophets."
>
> In the earliest Christian communities, on the other
> hand, one of the most marked features was the revival of
> prophecy.... But as in Israel, the church found its
> prophets often enough self-seeking and in one way and
> another "false" and devised ways to test them, primarily
> by their "fruits." The *Didache,* or *Teaching of the Twelve
> Apostles* (early second century), warns that "not everyone
> who speaks in a spirit is a prophet, except he have the
> behaviour of the Lord. From his behaviour, then, the
> false prophet and the true prophet shall be known" (7:8).

Without this background we might see only a prudential
warning and miss Jesus' assumption that prophecy has returned.
Likewise, without an outline of Jewish belief such as Linnemann's
(51–52) for the Good Samaritan (Lk 10:25–37), we might understand the lawyer's "Who is my neighbor?" simply as "Can't I draw
the line somewhere?"—not realizing that the question had a standard answer that the lawyer apparently intends to elicit but that
Jesus rejects.

Theological beliefs can be a key to Jesus' characterizations—
in the Lost Son (Lk 15:11–32), for example.

INTERPRETIVE MODEL

Linnemann, 75–76

> We are tempted to say, "What else should the man have
> done other than what he did when he was destitute?

When he went to a citizen of the land at least he
wanted to work." The pharisaic scribe would say, "He
should have worn his feet sore until he came to the
nearest Jewish community, and should have asked there
for help and work." This way he adds apostasy from the
faith of his fathers to his immoral life, since for him, living with a citizen of a foreign, gentile country, there can
be no Sabbath, no ritual eating, etc. Even the work
which this gentile employer gives him means for him a
sin. . . . He must have been . . . practically forced to
renounce the regular practice of his religion.

The picture of the son is here painted in gloomy
colours. He really is a lost son. The allusion to the tax-
collectors, to those who have renounced the laws of
their fathers' religion and gone into the service of the
gentiles, is now obvious.

Readers who are ignorant of Jewish law may not think of the
prodigal as foolish and impious for accepting what employment is
available.

Even our understanding of a plot may depend on the theological perspectives of the audience. In the Unjust Judge (Lk 18:1–
5) it helps to know that "The triadic formula 'widows, orphans, and
foreigners' summarizes in the Hebrew Bible the need of special
protection" (Scott, 181).

INTERPRETIVE MODEL

Scott, 182

Behind the pleadings of a widow lie potentially tragic
results. There is no welfare system, no safety net, to fall
back on if the judge fails to provide the special protection needed. In a subsistence world like Palestine, death
is not an unknown answer to a plea.

Reminded of this Old Testament teaching, we can hardly doubt the judge's responsibility to keep the story from having an unhappy ending.

EXERCISE

Exercise on the Pharisee and the Publican (Lk 18:9–14)

What is the theological basis of the judgment against the Pharisee (v 14)? Interpreters do not agree about the attitude reflected in the Pharisees' words or implied by Jesus' introduction, since, as Bailey says (1980, 147): "The phrase *pros heauton* can be read 'by himself' and attached to the previous word 'stood,' which gives us the above translation ['The Pharisee stood by himself thus praying']. Or it can be read 'to himself' and attached to the word 'praying' which follows. In this latter case it then reads, 'The Pharisee stood praying thus to himself.'" Consider the information in the following excerpts, along with other evidence of Jesus' conflict with the Pharisees (e.g., Lk 5:17–26; 6:1–11; 7:36–50; 11:37–44; 14:1–24; 15:1–16:31), and decide for yourself what brings Jesus' judgment on the Pharisee.

Scott (95–96) defends the Pharisee.

It is a prayer of thanksgiving.... The following prayer ... occurs in the Gemara as an example of the Mishnah command to pray on entering and leaving the house of study....

> I give thanks to Thee, O Lord my God, that Thou has[t] my portion with those who sit in the Beth ha-Midrash [the house of study] and Thou hast not set my portion with those who sit in [street] corners for I rise early and they rise early, but I rise early for words of Torah and they rise early for frivolous talk; I labour and they labour, but I labour and receive a reward and they labour and do not receive a reward; I run and they run, but I run to the life of the future world and they run to the pit of destruction.

The structure of this prayer is similar to that of the Pharisee. The Talmud does not view the prayer as self-righteous or boasting. The rabbi is giving God thanks that he has been so blessed by God as to be able to study the Torah....

Our inherited Christian map blocks us from seeing that in the Pharisee's own context his prayer depicts him as the ideal pious man.

Bailey (1980) makes the following points against the Pharisee.

1. "The Pharisee's reasons for standing apart can be easily understood.... Those who kept the law in a strict fashion were known as 'associates' (*haberim*). Those who did not were called 'people of the land' (*am-haaretz*)" (148).

2. "In the eyes of a strict Pharisee the most obvious candidate for the classification of *am-haaretz* would be a tax collector.... If he accidentally brushes against the tax collector ... he would sustain *midras*-uncleanness" (148).

3. "The great Hillel ... said, 'Keep not aloof from the congregation and trust not thyself until the day of thy death, and judge not thy fellow until thou art thyself come to his place' (Mishna *Pirke Aboth* 2:5, Danby, 448)" (149).

4. "Prayer in Jewish piety involved primarily the offering of thanks/praise to God for all of His gifts, and petitions for the worshiper's needs" (150).

5. "Moses stipulated a fast for the day of atonement (Lev. 25:29; Num. 39:7). This man goes far beyond" (152).

6. "Regarding the tithe, the Old Testament regulation was clear and limited. Tithes were levied on grain, wine, and oil (Lev. 27:30; Num. 18:27).... The practice of tithing nonagricultural products was just beginning to appear.... But this Pharisee—well, he tithed *everything*.... His acts are works of supererogation (Jeremias, *Parables*, 140). Amos had some sharp words for this type of religion (cf. Amos 4:4)" (152).

For another interpretive model on this parable, see Downing (80–94).

JEWISH HISTORICAL KNOWLEDGE

Jesus could choose the vehicle of analogy from his audience's experience either of past history or of current events, by the highly efficient technique of *allusion*—a passing reference to something in their store of experience. Whereas a hypothetical or fictional instance such as the Lost Son has to be spelled out in detail, Jesus has only to say "Jonah" or "Solomon," "Noah" or "Lot" (e.g., Mt 12:39–42; Lk 17:26–30) and instantly Jewish hearers have in mind a vivid, detailed image that he can apply immediately to his purpose. Or he can speak in a way that draws on their history less obviously, as in Mark 3:23–26.

INTERPRETIVE MODEL

Drury, 48

> The divided kingdom or house evokes the historic division of Israel and Judah after Solomon with all its dismal consequences familiar to Bible readers. The strong man recalls Isaiah 49:24f.:
>
> > Can the prey be taken from the mighty,
> >   or the captives of a tyrant be rescued?
> > Surely, thus says the Lord:
> >   "Even the captives of the mighty shall be taken,
> >   and the prey of the tyrant shall be rescued."

For his more alert Jewish hearers, Jesus' point is enriched by a concrete instance of most sacred significance. (Religious history is such a force for the Jews because it is the ground of both communal and personal identity.) The "dismal consequences" of division after Solomon's reign strongly emphasize this negative instance as Jesus reduces his opponents' accusation to absurdity. The Strong Man Bound (Mk 3:27), then, is a dramatic shift in tone from the tragedy of biblical history to hope, and all the more if we catch the scriptural allusions; Isaiah 49:24ff. (and 53:12) are bright promises of God's dealings with His people, illuminating the true significance of Jesus' exorcisms (in the synoptic parallels), that "The kingdom of God has come upon you" (Mt 12:28; cf. Lk 11:20).

The same goes for current events (e.g., Lk 13:1–5) or recent events, as Jeremias shows (59) in the Pounds (Lk 19:11–27).

> [In 4 B.C.] Archelaus journeyed to Rome to get his kingship over Judaea confirmed; at the same time a Jewish embassy of fifty persons also went to Rome in order to resist his appointment. The sanguinary revenge inflicted upon the people by Archelaus after his return had never been forgotten; Jesus appears to have used this incident in a crisis-parable as a warning to his audience against a false sense of security.

Here one tenor has two vehicles; one is *historical.*

> divine judgment : the unprepared = Archelaus' vengeance : his opponents
> with respect to retribution for rebellion

The *narrative* vehicle is complementary and reinforcing.

> divine judgment : the unprepared = new king's vengeance : his enemies
> with respect to retribution for rebellion

In the hearer's imagination the historical symbol of Archelaus creates an effect of pure terror; while the narrative symbol of the king, with his rewards as well as punishments, adds a strong motivation of hope.

EXERCISE

Exercises on the Murdered Galileans and the Victims of Siloam (Lk 13:1–5) and the Strong Man Bound (Mk 3:26–27)

1. What does Jesus gain by tapping his audience's recent memories of two tragedies, the natural disaster of a tower's collapse

and the political disaster of a governor's repression? Explore the effects on both tone and theme.

2.   The narrative and historical analogies in the Divided Kingdom, as Drury inteprets it (above), could be summarized thus:

(1) Satan casting out demons : Satan's rule = civil war: a kingdom
with respect to evidence of disintegration

(2) Satan casting out demons : Satan's rule = Jeroboam's rebellion : Rehoboam's united Israel
with respect to evidence of disintegration

Construct two proportional equations using the same tenor but different vehicles, to express Drury's interpretation of the narrative and historical analogies in the Strong Man Bound—in light of Isaiah 53:12. Explore the effects of the combination on both tone and theme.

For more information on the specifically Jewish background of the parables, see Oesterley.

TRADITIONAL STORIES AND MOTIFS

A shared stock of stories and folk motifs is also a part of the audience's mental equipment. Jesus may simply borrow something, or he may surprise his audience, playing off their expectations, as Jeremias (200) suggests about the Hidden Treasure (cf. part 2.4), and Scott about the Lost Son (Lk 15:11–32).

INTERPRETIVE MODEL

Scott, 112

Younger sons frequently leave the house of their father to find their wealth; there is something slightly

> scandalous or off-color in their stories; and they are the
> favorites. The story of Benjamin illustrates this final
> point. . . . Beyond the patriarchs this type of story per-
> sists. Aaron and Moses are elder and younger brothers,
> and David and Solomon are younger sons. Two of
> David's elder sons, Absalom and Adonijah, seek to seize
> David's throne, but Solomon, the youngest, the son of a
> wife whose husband David has murdered, becomes
> God's anointed king.

The stereotype or "mytheme" of the roguish but favored younger
son, Scott shows, is a well-established Jewish motif. Jesus exploits
it first by casting doubt over the customary expectation of restoration, secondly by fulfilling it dramatically in the father's welcome,
and finally—for the sake of his rejoinder to the Pharisees (Lk
15:1–2)—by suspending it at the end with the elder son's silence.

EXERCISE

Exercise on the Rich Man and Lazarus (Lk 16:19–31)

The Palestinian Talmud story of Bar Maayan, which lies
behind Jesus' parable of the Great Supper (cf. part 2.4), may also
have supplied Jesus with materials for the Rich Man and Lazarus
(quoted here from Scott, 157).

> There were two holy men in Ashquelon, who would eat
> together, drink together, and study Torah together. One of
> them died, and he was not properly mourned. But when Bar
> Maayan, the village tax collector, died, the whole town took
> time off to mourn him. The surviving holy man began to weep
> saying, "Woe, for the enemies of Israel [a euphemism for Israel
> itself] will have no merit." [The deceased holy man] appeared
> to him in a dream, and said to him, "Do not despise the sons of
> your Lord. This one did one sin, and the other one did one
> good deed, and it went well for [the latter on earth, so while

on earth I was punished for my one sin, he was rewarded for his one good deed]." Now what was the culpable act that the holy man had done? Heaven forfend! He committed no culpable act in his entire life. But one time he put on the phylactery of the head before that of the hand [which was an error]. Now what was the meritorious deed that Bar Maayan, the village tax collector, had done? Heaven forfend! He never did a meritorious deed in his life. But one time he made a banquet for the councillors of his town, but they did not come. He said, "Let the poor come and eat the food, so that it not go to waste." There are those who say that he was traveling along the road with a loaf of bread under his arm, and it fell. A poor man went and took it, and the tax collector said nothing to him so as not to embarrass him. After a few days the holy man saw his fellow [in a dream] walking among gardens, orchards, and fountains of water. He saw Bar Maayan the village tax collector with his tongue hanging out, by a river. He wanted to reach the river but could not reach it.

Assume that Jesus and his audience knew this version of the story. The parable preserves two of its essentials: a rich man's and poor man's reversal of fortunes between this life and the next, and the idea of this outcome being made known to someone in the story who is still in this world. Describe what Jesus' alterations accomplish, for both tone and theme, by exploiting the hearers' expectations.

See also Scott's discussion of various other parables, and Bauckham (225–46) on the Rich Man and Lazarus.

TRADITIONAL SYMBOLS

Modern notions of "creativity" as being radically innovative have prejudiced some modern readers against old stories and old symbols, but the Wedding Feast (Mt 22:1–14) shows how useful familiarity can be.

INTERPRETIVE MODEL

Drury, 98

Much of the allegorical symbolism is second-hand. It usually is, and is best that way because people will understand its signals. Jesus as bridegroom and his disciples as wedding guests goes back to Mark 2.19‖ Matthew 9.15. The king is God. What the burning of the city meant in terms of Jewish history could not be mistaken by anyone after AD 70. The guests who refuse their invitations are the Jews. Those who accept are Christians, 'bad and good' as Matthew knew them in his imperfect church. Likewise Wisdom had laid a banquet and invited the simple or 'foolish' (LXX) to eat it and become wise (Proverbs 9.1–6). In the background of the parable there is also the story of Esther, particularly the climactic banquet at the end of the tale where the unworthy Haman was unmasked and condemned.

Jesus has created a new combination of old symbols. Two in Drury's list involve Jesus' own words: the bridegroom and guests from another parable, the king from Jesus' teaching of the Kingdom. Two are Old Testament texts: of Wisdom's figurative banquet and Esther's literal one. To these traditional symbols are added new historical ones: the destruction of Jerusalem and the diverse reception of the gospel by Christians and by non-Christian Jews. Tapping the hearer's mind for just one key association can give a parable its power; here Jesus makes the imagination reach out in several directions at once.

A single powerful symbol can help one choose the main point of a parable from among several significant ones. In the Great Supper (Lk 14:15–24) "Jesus' use of the metaphor of a banquet would quite naturally have been interpreted eschatologically as a reference to the messianic banquet" (Stein, 86). Stein's numerous and diverse precedents show that the symbolic association is indeed traditional and thus probably familiar to Jesus' audience. Obviously the symbols should not be divorced from the Jews' agrarian culture, their perspective on history, and their theology of the end times. We must consider all these things when trying to determine what Jesus' audience brought with them to their hearing and how that mental equipment would have influenced their response.

Jesus finds a quite different use for the harvest symbol in the Rich Fool (Lk 12:13–21).

INTERPRETIVE MODEL

Scott, 138–39

> The parable implicitly invokes the kingdom of God in the harvest figure, for the miraculous harvest stands for (i.e., it is a metaphor for) the kingdom, representing God's blessing—a miracle. Its very size hints at both the tradition of a sabbatical year and Joseph's overseeing of Pharaoh's surplus and lean years. Ominously its bountifulness suggests a lean future, as both the literary parallels and the notion of limited goods indicate. While the harvest is an established metaphor for the kingdom, its very size implies the kingdom's intervention or coming.

From this example it is obvious that a traditional symbol may have not just one fixed meaning, but opposite meanings. Scott (332–33) cites an array of Old Testament texts to show that the Budding Fig Tree (Mk 13:28–29; Mt 24:32–33; Lk 21:29–31) and the Barren Fig Tree (Lk 13:6–9) rely on parallel traditions of the fig as a symbol of either blessing or cursing. So too in the Leaven (Mt 13:33).

INTERPRETIVE MODEL

Gundry, 268–69

> Usually leaven symbolizes the pervasive power of evil (Exod 12:15–20; 23:18; 34:25; Lev 2:11; 6:10[17]; Matt 16:5–12; 1 Cor 5:6–8; Gal 5:9). But sometimes it is associated with what is good (Lev 7:13–14; 23:17). Here, the unusual use of leaven with a good association not only emphasizes the point of the parable—the pervasive power of the kingdom of heaven—but also, and perhaps intentionally, agrees with the inclusion of publicans and sinners in the kingdom.

Accounting for this "unusual use of leaven" implies a comparison with the Leaven of the Pharisees (Mt 16:5–12), where leaven has its usual sinister meaning.

EXERCISE

Exercises on the Tenants (Mk 12:1–12; Mt 21:33–46; Lk 20:9–19), the Lost Sheep (Mt 18:12–14; Lk 15:3–7), and the Good Shepherd (Jn 10:11–18)

1. Explore the traditional symbolism of the vineyard by studying Deuteronomy 8:8; 1 Kings 4:25; 2 Kings 18:32; Canticles 8:11–13; Jeremiah 12:10; and the whole of Isaiah 5 (not just the "Song of the Vineyard," vv 1–7). Note the different symbolic meanings attached to the vineyard. Consider also the audience's acculturation in theology, in history, and in general. Which Old Testament texts seem pertinent to Jesus' parable? Why? What does traditional symbolism contribute to the tone and theme of the parable in the minds of Jesus' hearers? How might Jesus' omissions, additions, combinations, and other changes further affect his audience?

2. Explore the traditional symbolism of shepherd and sheep by reading Numbers 27:17; 1 Kings 22:17; 2 Chronicles 18:16;

Psalms 23:1–6; 79:13; 80:1–2; 95:7; 100:3; 119:176; Isaiah 40:11; 53:6; Jeremiah 23:1–6; 31:10; 50:6; Ezekiel 34:1–31. Note any variations in the symbolic meanings attached to this image in various texts. Answer the above questions for both versions of the Lost Sheep and for the Good Shepherd.

For additional interpretive models see Beavis, 1992, on servant parables and Jeremias (117–18) on the Patched Garment and the Wineskins (Mk 2:21–22).

ARCHETYPAL SYMBOLS

Jungian psychology suggests that some symbols are much more universal than the mental associations customary to a single people such as the Jews. Out of common experiences of human life, people everywhere seem to share certain images of the unconscious mind—death and rebirth preeminently. It follows that these images will recur spontaneously in certain literary plots, characters, and descriptive details; and that, as *archetypes*, they resonate in the imagination more deeply than ordinary "types" or symbols.

This theory of archetypes could help explain the symbolic force of the Budding Fig Tree (Mk 13:28–29).

INTERPRETIVE MODEL

Jeremias, 119–20

The fig-tree putting out its leaves is a sign of the coming blessing (Joel 2.22). The simile was intended by Jesus to direct the minds of his disciples . . . towards the signs of the time of salvation. The fig-tree is distinguished from the other trees of Palestine, such as the olive, the ilex, or the carob, by the fact that it casts its leaves, so that the bare spiky twigs which give it an appearance of being utterly dead, make it possible to watch the return of the rising sap with special clearness. Its shoots, bursting with life out of death, a symbol of the great mystery of death and life, herald the summer. In like fashion, says Jesus, the Messiah has his harbingers. Consider the signs: the dead fig-tree is clothed with green, the young shoots sprout, winter is over at last, summer is at the threshold, those destined for salvation awake to new life (Matt 11.5), the hour is come, the final judgment has begun, the Messiah is knocking at the door (Rev 3.20).

Jeremias is describing an archetypal image: in Israel the fig tree would be an apt symbol of the recurring cycle of death and life in the seasons of the year. This archetype involves a strong sense of the unwavering dependability of physical cycles, as expressed in God's promise to Noah: "As long as the earth endures, seedtime and harvest, cold and heat, summer and winter, day and night will never cease" (Ge 8:22). That suits Jesus' theme in the Budding Fig: the certainty of the Son of man's return "when you see these things happening."

> signs of times : expectation of Son of man = budding fig
> tree : expectation of summer
> with respect to *certainty of consequence*

Many of Jesus' images involve the cycle of the seasons, from the Tree and Its Fruit (Mt 7:15–20) to the Tenants (Mk 12:1–12), the Weeds (Mt 13:24–30) to the Rich Fool (Lk 12:13–21). Sometimes images of life and death come in clusters (Sider 1993, 430):

In Mark 4, symbols of flourishing life reinforce one another: the Sower, the Growing Seed, the Mustard Seed. In all these, moreover, the divine qualities of the kingdom stand out more sharply against the demonic archetypes of chapters 3 and 5:

the diseases of shriveled hand and hemorrhage (3:1, 5:25), the evil spirits (3:11, 5:1), destruction by drowning (4:38, 5:13) and the horror of a child's death (5:35).

Commenting on the Good Samaritan (Lk 10:25–37), Scott (189–90) remarks that "the temptation to draw the line, to dare someone to step across it, seems to be a universal human phenomenon." It frequently becomes a *plot-motif* in literature—here not in the plot of Jesus' parable, but in the plot of Luke's story, in which the lawyer draws a line limiting the law of love and Jesus steps across it. This is one important reason for the perennially compelling effect of the Good Samaritan (Donahue, 134):

> This parable is a "classic," that is, "any text, event or person which unites particularity of origin and expression with a disclosure of meaning and truth, available in principle to all human beings." It challenges us to move beyond our social and religious constructs of good and evil; it subverts our tendency to divide the world into insiders and outsiders.

Other archetypes in the parables include the Paradise-Hades image in the Rich Man and Lazarus (Lk 16:19–31), the journey in the Lost Son (Lk 15:1–32), and God in the Rich Fool (Lk 12:13–21). Though God rarely makes a literal appearance as in the Rich Fool, the many "monarchic parables" (Funk 1982, 29–54) are dominated by the figure of a father, a master, or a king, who generally is an archetype of God. That is why spontaneously we tend to feel that "the figure who plays God's role in a narrative *mashal* is always above opposition and blame" (Gerhardsson, 334). To judge a monarchical character by strictly human standards (e.g., Scott, 274–78, on the Unmerciful Servant) may be to ignore an archetypal significance that Jesus intends.

Just what counts as an archetype? To avoid diluting the concept we should look for it in only two classes of image. One is a small circle of experiences that really must be universal to humanity, such as the cycle of life and death. These are fewer than our ethnocentric perceptions might suggest; probably the Fatal Woman, dangerously attractive to a man (with Eve as its proto-type in Hebrew tradition) seems like an archetype only in patriar-chal societies, where the significance of womanhood is defined mainly by males. Matriarchal societies might have a Fatal Man symbol instead; obviously neither Woman nor Man would be truly archetypal. The other class includes images that a people believes or senses to be universal experiences—such as the Fatal Woman in our culture. With reasonable cautions we can greatly enhance our understanding of the emotional force of the parables by watch-ing for archetypes.

EXERCISE

Exercises on the Grain of Wheat (Jn 12:20–26) and the Lost Son (Lk 15:11–32)

1. The Grain of Wheat is an archetype of death and rebirth. How is it pertinent to Jesus' point about himself? about his hearers (cf. vv 20–23, 27–33)?
2. Sibling rivalry and rebellion against parental authority are universal enough to function as archetypes. What does the force of these figures in the parable of the Lost Son contribute to its effectiveness?

See Jones (175–84) for archetypal interpretation of the Lost Son (Lk 15:11–32).

2

GENRES

Considerations of *genre* (i.e., any literary kind or category embodied in the parables) could be regarded as an "internal feature." Certainly we recognize a genre by its intrinsic characteristics. But for the practical purposes of interpretation, questions about genre draw us to external considerations. Classifying words of Jesus as "parables" says something about his audience's *acculturated expectations,* for any genre is a bundle of expectations. As children learn to expect different things of teachers, parents, and storekeepers, so we learn different expectations of tragedies, sonnets, and nursery rhymes—all extremely important for meaning. The expectations that give genre its significance for interpretation are one more kind of acculturation. We ask questions about the literary kinds of the parables not just to be sure what is a parable and what is not, but to adjust our expectations and responses. (Otherwise it is possible to go very far wrong with a text. I once felt greatly distressed by something in the newspaper because I thought it was Ann Landers' advice column; but it became outrageously funny when I realized it actually was Erma Bombeck's domestic satire.) Because Jesus' parables comprise more than one literary type, we need to ask of each kind: "Do our expectations of genre in the parables conform well enough to those of Jesus' first audience?"

Most parables embody at least one genre of content and one of form. As we recognize comic strips, sonnets, or stage plays by form rather than by content, so we recognize Jesus' parables by their common form—analogy. And as we recognize a satire by its content (though its form may be comic strip, sonnet, or stage play), so we recognize some of Jesus' parables as *proverb*, or *taunt*, or *riddle*, or *picaresque fiction*, or even (in the essential matter of plot) *tragedy*. Some parables belong to several genres, just as one person may be adult, French, female, spouse, attorney, senior citizen, mother, socialist, Catholic, and war veteran.

The following survey of genres that appear in Jesus' parables is not exhaustive. The most conspicuous omission, allegory, needs no separate discussion here, for (as we have seen) like irony it is not a literary genre (though we may call some whole works "allegories"), but a device of rhetoric that can appear in many genres.

OLD TESTAMENT *MESHALIM*

Our purpose with this topic is to see how Old Testament analogies prepared Jesus' hearers for the mode of thought involved in his analogies. There is much more precedent in the Old Testament for Jesus' parabolic method than is often acknowledged by scholars who emphasize the uniqueness of the parables in the Gospels.

The Hebrew *mashal* denotes a much broader range of literary types in the Old Testament than does *parabole* in the New Testament. The Hebrew word can mean "likeness," and thus sometimes it serves as a label for analogies. But whereas *parabole* in the Gospels denotes only analogy, *mashal* (pl. *meshalim*) covers a variety of sayings that are not analogies, such as the oracles of Balaam (e.g., Nu 23:7) and some proverbs. Thus when Jeremias (20) says *parabole* is the same sort of catch-all label in the Gospels as *mashal* is in the Old Testament, he has not noticed that in the

Gospels it always means "analogy," or that the Septuagint typically translates *mashal* as *parabole* where analogy is involved (Sider 1981, 457–58).

MASHAL As SIMILITUDE

The Hebrew *mashal* apparently had to do originally with "likeness," e.g., Job 41:33, on the leviathan: "Nothing on earth is his *equal*—a creature without fear." As applied to language, perhaps it first denoted "analogy" in the sense of verbal comparison with a field of meaning including sayings like Jesus' short parables, which since Jülicher have been designated by the term *similitude* from Aristotle's *Rhetoric*. We shall see that analogy-*meshalim* function specially as riddle, proverb, taunt, or byword. Others are simply similitudes, e.g., the Forest Fire in Ezekiel 20:45–49 (labeled *mashal* in v 49). Drury (10) notes that Ezekiel is "complaining bitterly, 'Ah, Lord God! They say of me, is he not a speaker of parables?'—meaning that which is barely, if at all, intelligible." But Ezekiel's hearers may not have meant that he was unintelligible. If they could not follow the analogy of the Forest Fire, one wonders how hard they tried to understand. Perhaps instead their complaint means that, compared with straightforward discourse, parables are trivial—as the NIV suggests: "They are saying of me, 'Isn't he just telling parables?'" Either way *allegory* (v 49) is an appropriate label for this oracle, which is an extended metaphor framed by literal statements.

The rhetorical form of the Forest Fire is much like that of the Good Shepherd (Jn 10:11–18), midway in structure between Jesus' briefest similitudes and his story-parables: a literal introduction, followed by extended metaphor and mixed literal and figurative speech, and a literal conclusion. In mixed literal and figurative speech I have added quotation marks to distinguish the figurative elements.

Ezekiel 20:45–49	John 10:11–17

Literal Introduction

The word of the LORD came to me: ... "Son of man, ... say to the southern forest: 'Hear the word of the LORD. This is what the Sovereign LORD says: I am about to	I am

Extended Metaphor

set fire to you, and it will consume all your trees, both green and dry. The blazing flame will not be quenched, and every face from south to north will be scorched by it.	the good shepherd. The good shepherd lays down his life for the sheep. The hired hand is not the shepherd who owns the sheep. So when he sees the wolf coming, he abandons the sheep and runs away. Then the wolf attacks the flock and scatters it. The man runs away because he is a hired hand and cares nothing for the sheep.

Mixed Literal and Figurative Speech

Everyone will see that I the LORD have "kindled" it; it will not be "quenched." '"	I am the good "shepherd"; I know my "sheep" and my "sheep" know me—just as the Father knows me and I know the Father—and I lay down my life for the "sheep." I have other "sheep" that are not of this "sheep pen." I must bring them also. They too will listen to my voice, and there shall be one "flock" and one "shepherd."

Literal Conclusion

Then I said, "Ah, Sovereign LORD! They are saying of me, 'Isn't he just telling parables?'"	The reason my Father loves me is that I lay down my life—only to take it up again.

The parallel breaks down in the conclusion, where a new voice creates the shift to literal speech in Ezekiel; otherwise the *rhetorical* affinities are very close. Most important, the underlying *logical structures* are identical.

(1) God's judgment : Israel = wildfire : forest
with respect to swift destruction

(2) Jesus : disciples = shepherd : sheep
with respect to sacrificial care

Scholars who regard the Johannine parables as less authentic than those in the Synoptics should not overlook the significant Old Testament precedents for the form and logic of sayings such as the Good Shepherd.

Many *meshalim*-analogies are discourses of the sort found in Psalm 23: literal speech mixed with the figurative language of a recurring image, sometimes telling a kind of story (cf. Mt 5:13–16, Salt of the Earth and Light of the World; Jn 10:11–18, the Good Shepherd; Jn 15:5–8, the Vine and Branches). The familiar story-picture of Psalm 23 so dominates our imagination that we may need to be reminded just how thoroughly this psalm mixes literal language with figurative (the latter again distinguished in quotation marks).

The LORD is my "shepherd," I shall lack nothing.
   He makes me "lie down in green pastures,"
he "leads me beside quiet waters,"
   he restores my soul.

> He "guides me in paths" of righteousness
> for his name's sake. . . .

Some scholars acknowledge only a few "parables" in the Old Testament. They may not have noticed the multitude of rhetorical and logical parallels to Jesus' similitudes (see appendix B). Added to a number of full-fledged story-parables in the Old Testament, this range of analogy-*meshalim* corresponds to the whole scope of Jesus' parabolic sayings. Therefore in the form of his parables we find very little that his Jewish audience would not have recognized as entirely familiar from their scriptures. The challenges that confronted them in the parables came not from Jesus' method, but from his message.

Before turning to the story-parables of the Old Testament, in order to account for the expectations of Jesus' audience we must note how analogy is combined in some *meshalim* with other genres: riddle, proverb, taunt, and byword.

MASHAL AS RIDDLE

The Divided Kingdom (Mk 3:22–26) and the Strong Man Bound (Mk 3:26–27) carry on the Old Testament tradition of *mashal* as riddle. Drury characterizes the expectations that go with riddling in the Old Testament, and shows how they help explain this parable.

INTERPRETIVE MODEL

Drury, 16, 48

> Parables have been noticed to have a riddling character, being virtually synonymous with riddles at Ecclesiasticus 39.3 and 47.15. The classic biblical riddle is Samson's power at Judges 14.14,
>
> > Out of the eater came something to eat.
> > Out of the strong came something sweet.

The answer is the honeycomb which Samson had found in a lion's carcase. The riddle, like a figurative parable, presents a thing in an appropriate but abnormal way—in code. . . .

Which side is Jesus on, God's or the devil's? He is cornered in the house by the crowds and his hostile family and has to answer. So he does: but in parables. The dominant meaning of parable here is "riddle." A riddle seizes the initiative, allows the one put on the spot to put his interrogators on the spot. By resort to absurdity it pin-points the absurdity of the opposition. Riddle is the most aggressive kind of parable: little, hard, and menacing. The figures in these parables come from the Old Testament, baiting the trap with familiar reference.

The riddling analogies of the Divided House and Strong Man Bound respond to a challenge by putting the opponents on the defensive.

These parables are a shade more obscure than the usual image of Jesus, which Dodd describes as "leaving the mind in sufficient doubt about its precise application to tease it into active thought" (1935, 16). But they are not as obscure as the Sower (Mt 13:3–9), the Weeds (Mt 13:24–30), the Leaven of the Pharisees (Mt 16:5–12), and the analogy of Clean and Unclean (Mt 15:10–20), which naturally mystified the disciples. At twelve Jesus could already make people ponder with a riddling analogy (Lk 2:48–51). So his talk of rebirth and living water stimulated constructive questions from Nicodemus and the woman of Sychar (Jn 3:4; 4:11). "Destroy this temple" (Jn 2:19) shows that the method was lost on those whose questions were insincere. The riddle of the Sower tested the hearers' sincerity. Those outside excluded themselves voluntarily; on the other hand, "The Twelve and the others around him" (4:10), in Mark's unique phrase, were sincere enough to penetrate the initial bafflement of an obscure anecdote. Persistence, after all, is the theme of the gospel interpretation of the Sower—which has often been judged a secondary addition to Jesus' words by the same scholars who do not recognize the Old Testament tradition of *mashal* as riddle in such parables.

EXERCISE

Exercises on Clean and Unclean (Mk 7:7–23; Mt 15:10–20) and the Tenants (Mt 21:33–46)

1. What is Jesus' apparent special purpose for riddling with his disciples in the parable of the Clean and Unclean?
2. Gundry (427) says: "Jesus' consciousness of unique divine sonship—a consciousness that pervades the gospel tradition—supports his meaning himself in the figure of the son. Doubtless the audience's understanding did not measure up to Jesus' self-understanding." Why would Jesus convey his claims in this riddling fashion? Consider Matthew 21:42–46; 21:23–32; and 26:59–66.

MASHAL AS PROVERB

Some proverbs are figurative because they become analogies whenever we apply them. "A stitch in time saves nine," as applied to stopping a rumor before it spreads implies something like the following:

> early rumor-control : belated rumor-control = immediate mending : deferred mending
> with respect to the difference in the damage involved

Likewise, "For want of a shoe the horse was lost."

Some proverbs make an analogy with an old story. Thus accusing someone of "sour grapes" originates with Aesop's fox, which leaped in vain at a bunch of grapes, then consoled himself: "They're probably sour." So too with a proverb about Saul, and quite possibly one from Ezekiel.

INTERPRETIVE MODEL

Drury, 9

1 Samuel 10.9–13 tells of an extraordinary alteration in Saul's behaviour after his anointing by Samuel. "God gave him another heart," and he became an ecstatic prophet. "What has come over the son of Kish?" people wondered; "Is Saul also among the prophets?" A "man of place answered" enigmatically "And who is their father?" Therefore, the narrative continues, "it became a parable [RSV 'proverb'], 'Is Saul also among the prophets?'" Clearly it is a parable of a figurative sort, applicable when anybody behaves out of character.

Thus an actual occurrence can become proverbial by repeated application in new comparisons. So too with some of Jesus' images, such as serving two masters.

In its overlap with the proverb the *mashal* "has close affinities with the wisdom literature of the Old Testament, whose authors occasionally give it the meaning of a profound discourse upon a difficult problem (Job 27:1; 29:1; cf. Pss 49:4; 78:2)" (Mowry, 649). When studying literary context (part 3.3) and application to the original hearers (part 3.4) we should remember that when Jesus began telling a parable they may well have expected that kind of "wisdom."

Like other kinds of allusion the proverb instantly taps the hearer's memory. It evokes past situations that fit the proverb. Any parable makes a point vividly and memorably, but the allusiveness of a proverb-parable can double the force.

Not all of Jesus' proverbs are parables: "A prophet is not without honor" (KJV Mt 13:57; Mk 6:4; Lk 4:24); "The last will be first" (Mt 19:30; 20:16; Mk 10:31; Lk 13:30).

Exercise on "Physician, heal yourself" (Lk 4:23)

Luke calls this proverb a *parabole*. Consulting the context of the chapter, use proportions to work out the precise application to the situation Jesus is addressing, and the contributions to the effect of Jesus' whole commentary (4:22–30). Compare the formulas on pp. 70–71.

For another interpretive model see Noorda on "Physician, heal yourself."

MASHAL AS TAUNT

Drury's discussion of one Old Testament *mashal*-taunt defines the type and reminds us of at least one of Jesus' parables.

Drury, 13

A SONG OF DERISION

At Isaiah 14.4 a song of triumph over the fall of Babylon is introduced as a *mashal* (Septuagint, *thrēnos*). The cedars of Lebanon rejoice that they will not be cut down any more; the shades in Sheol welcome one as weak as themselves; Babylon is portrayed as a falling star. Habakkuk 2.6–8 and Micah 2.4 are much shorter examples, and less symbolically rich. But they too have a future orientation, the *mashal* as taunt performing the grand prophetic function of bringing history to a divine crisis which will change its course.

The Tenants (Mt 21:33–46) is Jesus' "taunt," with a "triumph" (v 42), against the Jewish elders, performing in verses 42–46 the same "grand prophetic function."

EXERCISE
_____

Exercise on the Places at Table and the Great Supper (Lk 14:7–11, 15–24)

Describe the effect, on both tone and theme, of those two parables taken as taunts in the Old Testament tradition.

MASHAL AS BYWORD

Some of Jesus' parables embody this type, represented in the Old Testament in Deuteronomy 28:37; Psalms 44:14; 69:11; 2 Chronicles 8:20; and Tobit 3:4 (Drury 13):

> Here the word "parable" is not applied to the intermediate literary or oral form but directly to the people or person in trouble—or about to be. They thereby "become parables," and the close connection of the parabolic and the historical is given another twist.
>
> At Deuteronomy 28.37 exile is prophesied in which the nation will "become horror" (Septuagint, *aenigma*), a *mashal/parabolē*, "and a byword among all the peoples where the Lord will lead you away." The same use is in the same context at Psalm 44.14. At Psalm 69.11 it is used of the lonely and derided righteous individual. At 2 Chronicles 8.20 it is used of the nation again, as at Tobit 3.4.

Could Luke's *parabolen pros autous legon* (12:16) possibly mean: "He described a byword for them"? As a terrible object lesson the rich fool has become a byword in Christian preaching. For Jesus and his audience the parable has both the spirit of the byword and its emotional coloring. The same may be said of the unmerciful servant (Mt 18:34), the one-talent man (Mt 25:28–30), the goats (Mt 25:41), the man clothed in purple (Lk 16:23–24), the victims of Pilate's massacre, and the people crushed by the tower of Siloam (Lk 13:1, 4).

EXERCISE

Exercise on the Ten Maidens (Mt 25:1–13)

How does one's consciousness of the Old Testament byword-*mashal* guide a reading of the fate of the five foolish maidens?

As riddle, proverb, taunt, or byword, parables of Jesus could recall some special associations that his audience attached to Old Testament *prophecy*. Fully to appreciate the parables' function in Jesus' prophetic ministry, we must weigh the effect produced by the connotations of these special kinds of *meshalim*. Most of the Old Testament story-parables following are prophetic oracles too.

OLD TESTAMENT STORY-PARABLES

The Old Testament has no distinguishing Hebrew label for its numerous story-analogies, but *story-parable* will do. None is labeled *mashal* except Ezekiel's symbolic narrative of the Cedar, the Eagles, and the Vine (17:1–24). (He also gives us the only concentration of true story-parables in the Old Testament.) This fantastic image does not remain a riddle for long. The prophet's tenor (vv 11–21) is Judah's foreign relations with Egypt and Babylon. Drury notes two elements that may point us to the expectations of Jesus' audience. First, Ezekiel's parable has the "stiffest historical grounding" (12) in the moment and purpose of his ministry; so too Jesus' audience must have expected his theme, not the story, to be the most important part. They would not hear the story as a free-standing artifact, as modern readers may be tempted to do. Second, Ezekiel's parable has "the beginnings" of an "apocalyptic vision of history" (13). On this precedent a Jewish audience might expect a parable to be eschatological.

Though Ezekiel's stories are often fantastic (e.g., both parables of chapter 19) they can be as realistic as any of Jesus' stories.

The rhetoric of the Watchman (33:2–6) allies it with hypothetical analogies like the Servant in Authority (Lk 12:42–46).

Ezekiel 33:2–6	Luke 12:42–46

Hypothesis

When I bring the sword against a land and the people of the land choose one of their men and make him their watchman, and he sees the sword coming against the land and blows the trumpet to warn the people,	Who then is the faithful and wise manager, whom the master puts in charge of his servants to give them their food allowance at the proper time?

Consequence

then if anyone hears the trumpet but does not take warning and the sword comes and takes his life, his blood will be on his own head. Since he heard the sound of the trumpet but did not take warning, his blood will be on his own head. If he had taken warning, he would have saved himself.	It will be good for that servant whom the master finds doing so when he returns. I tell you the truth, he will put him in charge of all his possessions.

Antithesis

But if the watchman sees the sword coming and does not blow the trumpet to warn the people and the sword comes and takes the life of one of them,	But suppose the servant says to himself, "My master is taking a long time in coming," and he then begins to beat the menservants and womenservants and to eat and drink and get drunk.

Consequence

that man will be taken away because of his sin, but I will hold the watchman accountable for his blood.	The master of that servant will come on a day when he does not expect him and at an hour he is not aware of. He will cut him to pieces and assign him a place with the unbelievers.

In Luke the explanation comes first (v 40): "Be ready." In Ezekiel it follows (vv 7ff.) "Son of man, I have made you a watchman."

Some Old Testament parables, like some of Jesus' parables, are responses to the actions of others. Jehoash's Thistle and Cedar (2Ki 14:7–10) is a rebuff like Jesus' reply to the disappointed heir in the story of the Rich Fool (Lk 12:13–21)—but a good deal rougher. The Trees (Jdg 9:7–21) is a desperate appeal by Jotham, Jerub-Baal's sole surviving son, to the citizens of Shechem after they helped his brother Abimelech murder his sixty-nine other brothers and made him king. No other Old Testament parable has so much narrative development: a dialogue with several speakers, a series of parallel episodes proceeding to a contrasting climax. The series exploits the rule of three (part 2.4): it heightens the suspense by paralleling the third tree's reply to the first two, and deferring the expected contrast to the fourth reply. And there are three points of resemblance.

Shechemites : Abimelech = trees : bramble
with respect to (1) invitation of last resort
                (2) consequent lack of good faith
                (3) consequent mutual enmity

Jotham's first point is implied in the trees' succession of fruitless appeals and the reduction to the lowly bramble; Abimelech is literally the last son of Gideon (Jerub-Baal) that one would choose as king. Second, the people of Shechem must therefore have no genuine respect for him; their allegiance is temporary expedience, not good faith. Third, the devouring fire is a prophecy of the inevitable result—a true prophecy as it turns out (vv 22–23). The reasons of the olive, fig, and vine for refusing to reign appear to be nonsymbolic details.

All the story-parables in the Old Testament have an explanation (though Amaziah could hardly miss the message of the Thistle and Cedar). Jesus' audience must have expected no less. We should not treat the explanations attached to the Sower and the Weeds (Mt 13:18–23, 36–43) as secondary additions to Jesus' words merely on the arbitrary theory that "the speaker who needs to interpret his parables is not master of his method" (Cadoux, 19). Some "morals" can be left unsaid, but many stories could illustrate diverse themes, and thus are far too ambiguous to stand without commentary.

Though the attractiveness of Jesus' plots and characters is universally praised, the antagonizing "mousetrap" effect of some parables is not so often acknowledged. Drury (12) calls Nathan's parable of David's sin against Uriah a mousetrap because that was Hamlet's word for the stage-play by which he replicated his murdering uncle's crime before his face. So too in Isaiah 5 God and the prophet purpose together to curse Judah and Israel, but to trap them first. The bait for the trap is the Song of the Vineyard describing how things should have been—how Judah and Israel presumably believe things actually are. After the Song has encouraged this false security, the trap catches them in their real situation before God. Some interpreters have doubted that Jesus' parable of the Tenants owes anything to Isaiah's Song because the disappointment in one case is the vines, and the vinedressers in the other. Yet the basic strategies are similar. The Jewish leaders are caught when an attractive image for Israel goes very sour indeed.

Jesus' audience would recognize this method not only from Isaiah's Song, but also Nathan's Ewe Lamb (2Sa 12:1–14), Joab's delegated story of the Two Brothers (2Sa 14:1–21), and a prophet's tale of the Escaped Prisoner (1Ki 20:35–43). Each of these replicates in analogy the misdoings of a king—indirectly, to forestall his wrath. Each is a fiction represented as fact to the king, whose judgment on it unavoidably applies to himself. "You are the man!" Nathan tells David. There are subtler traps in other parables of Jesus, especially the Vineyard Laborers (Mt 20:1–16) and the Rich Man and Lazarus (Lk 16:19–31), and a more obvious one in the Two Debtors (Lk 7:41–47).

EXERCISE

Exercises on the Ewe Lamb (2Sa 12:1–14) and the Lost Son (Lk 15:11–32)

1. What can we gather from Nathan's parable about the probable mindset of Jesus' audience toward his parables?
2. Jesus' mousetraps force a judgment from his audience about the vehicle of his analogy, leaving them to find themselves as its tenor. Explain the Pharisees' situation (cf. 15:1–2) at the father's final appeal in the Lost Son.

RABBINIC AND NEW TESTAMENT ANALOGUES

Rabbinic parables may also illuminate the expectations of Jesus' audience, even though none of the extant examples can be dated as early as the time of his ministry. Blomberg's evidence (59–64) that his method probably resembled the rabbis' helps further to define and corroborate our picture of what Jesus' audience expected of a parable.

1. The Rabbinic parables almost always begin with an introductory formula which parallels those found in the Gospels. . . .

2. Often the logic of [one] category of parable [beginning with the phrase "in the custom of the world"] is "from the lesser to the greater." ...
3. The length and structure of the rabbinic parables also resemble those of the parables of Jesus. ...
4. The parables of Jesus and the rabbis further share common topics and imagery. ...
5. The rabbis interpreted their parables in a variety of ways, but almost always with some allegorical element. ...
6. The purposes of the rabbinic parables involve both disclosure and concealment. ...

In this last point we see reflected the Old Testament tradition of *mashal* as riddle. See also Young on the rabbinic background of Jesus' parables.

Similar parallels exist between Jesus' parables and New Testament parables outside the Gospels, such as the Child Heir (Gal 4:1–11). In both logic and rhetoric there are also close affinities between Romans 7:2–3 and Luke 12:42–46; Romans 11:13–14, 23–24 and Matthew 7:15–17; 1 Corinthians 12:11–13a and Matthew 5:14–16; 1 Corinthians 14:7–9 and Matthew 7:16b, 20; James 2:14–17 and Luke 15:4–7. Many of these resemble some of Jesus' parables more than scholars commonly acknowledge. Even where the rhetoric is different from Jesus' rhetoric, as in Paul's "allegory" in Galatians 4:24 of Hagar and Sarah's songs—unique in the New Testament—the thought is composed of familiar forms of logic. To contrast the slavery of law with the freedom of faith (cf. 2:15–16), Paul makes several proportional analogies with the situations of Ishmael and Isaac. If the extant rabbinic parables are important despite their uncertain dating, the parables in Acts and the Epistles may be more so. For when the evangelists were handling the traditions of Jesus' parables they may have known these other parabolic materials. Their writings provide more opportunities for us to identify the customary expectations of Jesus' audience about analogies, and to adjust our expectations accordingly.

GREEK AND ROMAN FABLES

The last thing we wish, of course, is mistakenly to bring to the parables our own peculiar expectations that are inspired by a genre foreign to the culture of the time. As soon as we stray from the literary traditions of the Old Testament and the rabbis to the classical types of Greece and Rome we must accept the burden of proving that such genres were part of the mental equipment of Jesus' Jewish audience. But the classical *fable* probably influenced Jesus and his audience, as Jülicher noted (I, 98) and Beavis elaborates (494).

> Recent scholarship has made it increasingly clear ... that sharp distinctions between "Greek" and "Jewish" influences on early Christianity are suspect. . . . Both fable and *mashal* are descended from a common Near Eastern ancestor. Hellenistic influence on rabbinic teaching and literary forms is well documented. Our growing awareness of the extent of Hellenistic culture in Palestine forbids us to rule out the possibility of the influence, direct or indirect. As R. Funk observes, "It is not impossible that Jesus spoke Greek as well as Aramaic, and that the foundational language of the Christian tradition received its decisive imprint in Greek." The Synopticists, who wrote in Greek, and who almost certainly had at least a Greek elementary education, might well be expected to have further shaped the parables of Jesus into a well-known Greek popular literary class: the fable.

Beavis also points out (478–80) that it is a mistake to regard the classical fables as nothing more than animal stories since "a significant minority" have everyday human subjects. Such fables resemble Jesus' parables in important ways: (1) "both are brief, invented narratives"; (2) they "are not fantastic stories, but involve ordinary human characters and situations"; (3) they "have religious or ethical themes"; and (4) "despite their realism, the fables contain an element of extravagance." One of her examples (479–80) is from Phaedrus IV.8.

> When a certain man was complaining about his ill fortune, Aesop invented the following story to comfort him. A ship had been badly tossed about by fierce storms so that its passengers were in tears and fear of death, when suddenly the weather changed and took on a serene aspect; the ship began to ride to safety, borne along by favourable winds, which raised the spirits of the sailors to an excessive pitch of joy. Hereupon the pilot, made wise by danger in the past, remarked: "One must be cautious in rejoicing and slow to complain, for the whole of life is a blend of grief and joy."

There are further similarities between this Aesopian parable and many in both testaments: (5) The occasion, or *Sitz im Leben*, of the story is narrated separately (first sentence); and (6) the moral significance is summed up (last sentence), with a clearly implied application to the complaining man for whom the story was invented.

We can sharpen our instincts for the parables by exploring the classical fables. They will inform our expectations about analogy and allegory much more fully than would be possible if we read only the parables of Jesus, for they give us perspective and an invaluable basis for comparison.

OTHER LITERARY ANALOGUES

Many other kinds of literature can also contribute to this basis for comparison, which is indispensable to interpretation at its best. That is Lewis's point in the following appeal of a literary critic to biblical scholars (1967, 154).

> A man who has spent his youth and manhood in the minute study of New Testament texts and of other people's studies of them, whose literary experiences of those texts lack any standard of comparison such as can only grow from a wide and deep and genial experience of literature in general, is, I should think, very likely to miss the obvious things about them. If he tells me that something in a Gospel is legend or romance, I want to know how many legends and romances he has read, how well his palate is trained in detecting them by the flavour.

This critical faculty cannot be attained by reading literary theory; a full acquaintance with the genre of the parable requires wide reading of literature itself, with some discriminations about which "parables" are really like Jesus'. Kafka's short-story "parables," for example, cannot help us much. They are *freestanding* artifacts, and their meaning is open-ended—i.e., susceptible to the reader's free improvisation—whereas Jesus' parables are *embedded literary subsets* of his discourse and the evangelists' narrative, and their meaning is subject to the control of Jesus' authoritative intent.

The best literary parallels are "analogies with pictorial or narrative images, put to the service of discourse set in the context of some larger story" (Sider 1993, 427). Such analogies abound in various kinds of literature (Sider 1993, 427):

> from More's analogy of Seneca in comedy (*Utopia* 28–29) and Shakespeare's "vicious mole" (*Hamlet* 1.4.17–38) to Lincoln's borrowed proverb on the crisis of the Union: "A house divided against itself cannot stand" (Lincoln 429) and the Lord High Executioner's song of "Tit Willow" in *The Mikado* by Gilbert and Sullivan (395–96).

The genre of Jesus' parables is also replicated by many anecdotes and illustrations in sermons, speeches, and scientific demonstrations.

CHAPTER

3

LITERARY CONTEXTS

Besides the cultural contexts just explored, the parables have *textual* and *literary* contexts: the Gospels, the rest of the New Testament, and the Old Testament. For example, the Unmerciful Servant (Mt 18:23–35) should not be interpreted as a free-standing story because it is the *vehicle* of an analogy ("A king . . . wanted to settle accounts") attached to its *tenor* ("The kingdom of heaven is like . . .") within a *discourse* ("Lord, how many times shall I forgive my brother?") within a *story* of Matthew's ("Peter came to Jesus and asked . . .") within a *thematic unit* (Mt 18) of Matthew's gospel.

> gospel > thematic unit > story > discourse > analogy (tenor + vehicle)

NARRATIVE SECTION

Thus we find cues to interpretation of a parable in each enveloping literary structure, beginning with the *narrative section* in which it occurs, i.e., the immediate context of the evangelist's story of Jesus, with its characters, dialogue, and action. In the Great Supper (Lk 14:15–24) the contextual dialogue helps Stein choose between two possible main points. Is the emphasis on "vindication by Jesus to his critics of his preaching the good news to the poor and the outcasts of Israel" or on "proclamation that indeed the messianic banquet (or the kingdom of God) had come"?

INTERPRETIVE MODEL

Stein, 87

> The present context of our present parable ... favors an eschatological interpretation, for the setting given for the parable in v. 15 is a statement about the joy of participating in the bliss of the kingdom of God. The setting of Luke 14:15 is therefore not one in which Jesus must defend himself, but rather one in which he comments concerning the bliss of eating bread in the eschatological kingdom and the parable which follows should therefore be interpreted as teaching about that kingdom.

Stein concludes (89) that if one ignores the call to the arrival of the kingdom, "it will mean exclusion," even though the parable clearly vindicates Jesus' preaching to the poor and outcasts.

> God : sinners and Gentiles = householder : those from street and highway
> with respect to new invitation

For the parable is Jesus' response to a fellow guest's remark about the eschatological kingdom; therefore that is its main theme—in particular, the urgency of accepting the opportunity.

> those who ignore God's call : God = the original guests : the householder
> with respect to exclusion

The context of Jesus' *discourse* may be helpful too. Taken solely in the light of Mt 20:16 ("The last will be first, and the first will be last") the main point of the parable of the Vineyard Laborers might seem quite general.

> the self-righteous : the consciously needy = all-day workers : one-hour workers

with respect to reversal of relative status

But Jesus has just promised the disciples that they will "sit on twelve thrones, judging the twelve tribes of Israel" (Mt 19:28). As Donahue points out (84), the parable gives "a proper perspective" to this distinction:

> Though they have followed Jesus when first summoned (Matt 4:18–22), both the call and the reward are still in the hand of the householder. . . . The first may be last and the last first. God's generosity is equally present to those called last.

In other words:

(1) the sacrificial Twelve : other disciples = the day-long workers : the one-hour workers

with respect to essential equality

Donahue adds: "The promise . . . should not lead them to assume this role prematurely."

(2) the sacrificial Twelve : God = the day-long workers : the owner

with respect to danger of presumption

Jesus' prior words make the point more particular.

EXERCISE

Exercise on the Rich Man and Lazarus (Lk 16:19–31)

How does the preceding *dialogue* of 16:14–15 focus the meaning of the first part of the parable (vv 19–26)? How does the preceding *discourse* of 16:16–18 focus the meaning of the second part of the parable (vv 27–31)?

The evangelist's *narrative* may provide similar cues. For example, Moessner points from the parable of the Pounds (Lk 19:11–27) to the context of Luke's story.

INTERPRETIVE MODEL

Moessner, 171–72

Luke states (19:11) that the crowd of 19:3 (cf. 19:7b) heard Zacchaeus's confession and Jesus' affirmation (19:8–10). How ironic that the crowds still do not recognize the Kingdom in their midst. They suppose it is still to come, and because Jerusalem is within sight, its coming will be immediate as it appears in Jerusalem. Thus the crowd holds the identical view of the Kingdom as the Pharisees in 17:20–21: it is something that will appear in a convincing form; it is certainly not effective in Jesus' journeying in the present.

The thrust of Jesus' parable confirms this interpretation of the comment in 19:11. . . . The imagery of a nobleman and servants does not appear to stem from the journeying-guest mission. Yet these figures, within the journeying context of one in authority, fit admirably into the dramatic buildup of Jesus' own journey as guest. As with the citizens who hated the "nobleman-lord," so it becomes clear as Jesus approaches Jerusalem that his "citizens" "do not want this man to reign over us."

The people's expectation that "the kingdom of God was going to appear at once" (Lk 19:11) is crucial to understanding Jesus' intent in the parable.

EXERCISE

Exercises on the Sower (Mk 4:3–9, 14–20) and the Tenants (Mt 21:33–46)

1. Mark 4 is not just a collection of parables but a Markan narrative about Jesus' preaching with some illustrative examples.

What light does Mark's story in chapter 4 shed on Jesus' themes in the parable of the Sower?

2.   What light does Mt 21:1–22:46 shed on the Tenants through (a) various persons' dialogue, (b) Jesus' discourse, and (c) Matthew's narrative?

For more interpretive models see Kilgallen (1989) and Tolbert (1993).

GOSPEL

Obviously the evangelist includes parables that suit his gospel. The appropriateness of the Two Sons to Matthew's gospel (21:28–31) is part of its meaning.

INTERPRETIVE MODEL

Hunter, 54

> Once again, we have a rebuke of the Scribes and Pharisees. "They say and do not," was Jesus' verdict on them (Matt. 23.3), whereas he found that so-called reprobates like tax-gatherers and harlots, who made no pious claims, had a way of closing with God's call when it came to them.

Hunter points to another part of Matthew to illumine the main point of the Two Sons. As the second son said: "I will, sir," but didn't, so the scribes and Pharisees "say and do not."

Whereas Hunter appeals to the *pattern of ideas* in a gospel, Gundry invokes a *pattern of images* to explain the Sower (Mt 13:3–9; Mk 4:3–9; Lk 8:4–8).

INTERPRETIVE MODEL

Gundry, 254

> Concerning what fell on good soil, Matthew includes, as he must, the positive statement "and it was giving fruit." But he subtracts Mark's immediately following words, "coming up and growing, and it was bearing." The subtraction causes the emphasis to fall solely on the giving of fruit, a prominent metaphor in Matthew for works—here good works, obviously.

Gundry argues that Matthew's motive for the rhetorical emphasis is his concern for "works," both in the Sower and elsewhere, repeatedly referring to them as "fruit" (e.g., 3:10; 7:16–20; 12:33). Goulder (101–2) shows how extensive and various Matthew's image patterns can be.

A gospel's *pattern of history* may also be significant. For instance, in the reader's retrospect on the whole gospel, certain events are examples that parallel and reinforce the points of the Sower. Drury shows how the connections between the Sower (Mk 4:3–8) and the rest of Mark's gospel are not just philosophical and thematic, like the patterns above, but historical and predictive.

INTERPRETIVE MODEL

Drury, 51–52

> The birds which take away the word-seed ... are Satan ... (4.15). Now, Peter will be on the way with Jesus as his disciple at 8.27. But at 8.32 he will try to remove Jesus' prophecy of the doom, death and resurrection, of the Son of Man: to take away that word. It amounts to a cancellation of the gospel at its christological base. So Jesus will rebuke him with the words "Get behind me Satan! For you are not on the side of God, but of men"

(8.33). The parable's prophecy is fulfilled. Next in the interpretation comes the shallow and rocky ground which is said to represent those who "when tribulation or persecution arises on account of the word, immediately fall away" (4.17). This too will get its precise historical fulfillment. At 14.43 tribulation will arise as Judas and his posse come to arrest Jesus in the garden, and at 14.50 Mark says, "they all [the eleven] forsook him and fled." The third category is "the ones sown among thorns; they are those who hear the word, but the cares of the world, and the delight in riches, and the desire for other things, enter in and choke the word, and it proves unfruitful" (4.18f). At 10.17 Jesus will be accosted by a rich man eager to inherit eternal life. He tells him, "Go, sell what you have, and give to the poor, and you will have treasure in heaven; and come, follow me."

> At that saying [*epi tō logō* = on account of the word] his countenance fell, and he went away sorrowful; for he had great possessions.

The word of discipleship, 'follow me', was spoken to him. But it was strangled at birth by wealth.

So each occurrence in the parable has, via its interpretation, an exact equivalent in the narrative of the book. There is one striking exception, the good soil with its abundant crop. No one in the narrative reaches that happy condition. Mark would seem to be looking beyond his book, with its famously abrupt ending, to the life of his church; hoping for better things after the resurrection than happened before it.

This is a wonderfully illuminating synthesis of separate elements in Mark; such connections can be found between any parable and the rest of its gospel.

For additional interpretive models see Boucher on Mark and Kingsbury on Matthew.

OTHER PARABLES

Some books group the parables by image (e.g., Scott) and some by theme (e.g., Jeremias, Hunter, Crossan, Stein). Either way, one parable may help us understand another. We have noted doublets and triplets, and scattered parables that form a thematic system by their common theme (part 1.6). Donahue invokes Jesus' discourse both in parable and otherwise, linking larger groups of parables with Luke's nonparabolic materials, as well as other parts of the New Testament.

INTERPRETIVE MODEL

Donahue, 192–93

> Prayer has a manifold importance for Luke. It opens human beings to communion with God, and God becomes present at moments of prayer. Through prayer, Christians, to use Pauline language, take on the mind of Christ (Phil. 2:5). As Jesus prepares for important moments in following God's will, so too must the pilgrim community as it makes its way to the end of the earth. The early church is characterized by *koinonia* (communal life) expressed in the breaking of the bread, in prayer, and in concern for the poor in the community (Acts 2:42–47; cf. 4:32–37).
>
> The beginning and the end of the special material of Luke's travel narrative are marked by groups of parables (the Good Samaritan/Martha and Mary; the Friend at Midnight; the Unjust Judge/the Pharisee and the Tax Collector) in which prayer is central and which therefore anchor Jesus' teaching on "the way" of Christian

discipleship as he himself makes his "way" to Jerusalem. These parables, which shock the sensibilities of the hearers, open them to a new understanding of the way of discipleship. It comprises compassionate entry into the world of the suffering neighbor, along with the rhythm of listening to the word and quiet presence before God, just as a similar rhythm characterized Jesus and the early church. Prayer, however, does not lead to passive acquiescence to evil. Under persecution the early community pray for "boldness"; their prayer is answered and they confront brutal power. The exhortation "always to pray and not lose heart" (18:1) is illustrated by the story of a widow who aggressively seeks justice.

Donahue's method synthesizes our topics in part 3.3–4, including other parables, other gospel materials, the Pauline writings, and experience of the early church.

EXERCISE

Exercises on the Pharisee and Publican (Lk 18:9–14) and the Growing Seed (Mk 4:26–29)

1. Find passages in other parts of Luke (including parables) and in Acts that seem related to the situation of the Pharisee and the Publican; interpret the parable in their light.
2. Use Mark's whole "parable chapter" to identify the tenor of the Growing Seed. Pay special attention to complementary images of vegetative growth.

The broad possibilities for synthesizing parables and other features of the Gospels is illustrated in Moessner's expansive array of evidence (160–62) about the tenor of the Unjust Steward (Lk 16:1–13). He has a useful method of studying a parable's context: (1) survey the gospel for any similarities and contrasts to the parable, without much concern at first about their relevance; (2) discriminate the greater and lesser relevance of these similarities and contrasts; (3) assimilate the truly relevant affinities into the interpretation.

The parallel ideas and doctrines from other gospels can illumine a parable. Thus Hunter uses a Matthean parable to help explain one in Luke (55): "If The Two Sons says to the Scribes and Pharisees, 'The tax-gatherers and harlots are going into the Kingdom before you,' The Two Debtors says to an individual Pharisee, 'This "bad woman" is nearer to God than you are.'" Finding *similarities* between one gospel and another can help us understand the mind of Christ (or the church) about a parable; the preceding discussion deals with that. The *differences*, which speak rather to the mind of the evangelist, are the subject of redaction criticism (part 3.4).

See also Heard (65–66) and Parrott on parables in Luke.

THE NEW TESTAMENT

Because the mind of Christ and the church is reflected also in the whole New Testament, interpreters use this larger context of a parable as they do the Gospels. Hunter (63) notes Paul's way of stating Jesus' *theology* in the Lost Son (Lk 15:11–32). Donahue (77) cites James's language for Jesus' *ethics* in the Unmerciful Servant (Mt 18:23–35). The possibilities are virtually unlimited for making illuminating connections between the parables and almost everything else in the New Testament.

EXERCISE

Exercise on the Vineyard Laborers (Mt 20:1–16), the Rich Fool (Lk 12:13–21), and the Unjust Judge (18:1–8)

How do the following New Testament teachers help articulate Jesus' message in the parables: Paul (1Cor 12) for the Vineyard Laborers, James (4:13–16) for the Rich Fool, and the author of Hebrews (chap. 11) for the Unjust Judge?

See also Siker (73–74), for the relation of a parable to the rest of the New Testament.

THE OLD TESTAMENT

Jesus' parables frequently allude to the Old Testament. We have seen some examples (e.g., part 3.2), and Gundry suggests another allusion in the Sower (Mt 13:3–9, 18–23).

INTERPRETIVE MODEL

Gundry, 261

> It is possible that the path represents failure to hear by not loving God with the heart, the rocky soil failure to hear by not loving God with the soul (i.e., by not risking one's life for the word in times of persecution), and the thorny soil failure to hear by not loving God with might (i.e., with the sacrifice of one's material wealth)—all of this after the pattern of Deut 6:4–5.

For the hearer who makes the connection, the parable gains all the authority and atmosphere of an Old Testament motif that is fundamentally formative for Jewish faith and hope: the law of the Great Commandment.

Jesus can also draw on a powerfully evocative personal history, as in the Lost Son (Lk 15:11–32).

INTERPRETIVE MODEL

Drury, 144–45

> It is a parable ... full of echoes of the Joseph story. It too begins with the younger son who goes down to a far country where he is nearly caught by a harlot (Potiphar's wife), and where there was famine. It ends similarly. In Genesis 45 the son Joseph rushes to meet

his approaching father Israel and falls on his neck:
Luke's roles reversed. To the famine which occupies the
middle of both tales the protagonists react differently—
both shrewdly, but Joseph by provident administration
and Luke's man by smelling roast veal from afar and
"coming to himself." Pharaoh at Genesis 41.42 "took
his signet ring from his hand and put it on Joseph's
hand, and arrayed him in garments of fine linen." So
here at 15.22 the father says, "Bring quickly the best
robe and put it on him, and put a ring on his hand." We
are in the same world, or world-view. Here God
worked in and through the human causality of the tale
so implicitly as to be hidden in its continuum.

The parable invites us to grasp intuitively the symbolic force
of the similarities before reasoning them out. Joseph thus becomes
a standard for our judgment on the prodigal's failings.

Can we be sure that Jesus had these Old Testament stories
echoing in his mind? Would his audience recognize and appreciate
them? In discussing the Mustard Seed (Mk 4:30–32; Mt 13:31–
32; Lk 13:18–19), Crossan asks: Is Jesus' "allusion" here to texts
such as Psalm 104:12; Daniel 4:10–12; and Ezekiel 17:23; 31:6
just a reader's free association?

INTERPRETIVE MODEL

Crossan, 1973, 47–48

Because of these texts the commentators usually see in
the ending of the Mustard Seed parable a reference to
apocalyptic eschatology and its image of the end-time
as a great tree with birds nesting in its branches. But it
must be noted that in Daniel and Ezekiel the references
are to a great and mighty tree or to the majestic cedar
of Lebanon, and that there is always the parallelism of
nesting birds and resting beasts: the former are in the

branches; the latter are in the shade of the tree. Only Ps 104:12, which does not mention a *tree* at all and does not have this poetic parallelism of nesting birds and resting animals, would be a viable allusion for a parable concerning a mustard shrub which, as J. D. Kingsbury has noted, "cannot, by any stretch of imagination, be classified as a ... tree proper." ...

If there is any Old Testament allusion behind the original version of Mark 4:31, it is no more and no less than an allusion to God's loving providence in the pastoral scene of Psalm 104:12.

It is wise not to claim too much about Jesus' *intent* from a parable's similarity to something in the Old Testament. But the parable's *effect* on a hearer's free associations may be significant too; what matters is the real relevance of the connections we make. Without asserting that Jesus had the Old Testament in mind when he told the parable of the Mustard Seed, Crossan finds Psalm 104:12 truly pertinent: "The birds of the air nest by the waters; they sing among the branches."

EXERCISE

Exercises on the Lost Son (Lk 15:11–32), the Sower (Lk 8:5–15), and Job 31

1. What does Deuteronomy 21:18–21 suggest about Jesus' doctrine of God in the father's treatment of the prodigal?
2. All four of the sower's soils stand for hearers of the word (Lk 8:12–15). What do verses 9–10 suggest about this hearing? How does Ezekiel 12:1–2 and the whole of Isaiah 6 (not just 6:9–10) affect your answer? What about the last verses of Luke's second volume (Acts 28:23–28)?

3. To address Jesus' allusions to the Old Testament we should read it with the parables in mind. On which parables (at least three) does Job 31 shed very specific light?

Other Old Testament precedents for Jesus' parabolic images may be found in Job 20:28 (the Two Builders, Mt 7:24–27), Isaiah 8:19–20 (the Rich Man and Lazarus, Lk 16:19–31), Isaiah 56:12 (the Rich Fool, Lk 12:13–21), Jeremiah 4:3 (the Sower, Mk 4:3–8), and Jeremiah 39:1–7 (the Pounds, Lk 19:11–27).

See Kingsbury and Kistemaker for further numerous connections between the parables and the Old Testament; cf. Hunter (48–49) on the Strong Man Bound (Mk 3:26–27).

We must acknowledge not only that the whole meaning of a single parable depends partly on its literary context, but also that the meaning of the whole body of Jesus' parables likewise depends on context. Because of the parables' common basis in form, and in consideration of their special functions, it is appropriate to single them out of the Gospels for separate consideration—but only as a preliminary to interpreting them as an integral part of the whole body of Jesus' teaching, and the whole message of the Bible.

4

INTERPRETIVE CONTEXTS

Since interpretation is one reader helping another, we should note how others have responded to the parables, from Jesus' original hearers and the early church (as reflected in the Gospels and Epistles) to the great company of readers in successive ages. How should any audience hear the parables? Fuchs (207ff.) described the effect of the parable as "language-event," and Lambrecht (17) reminds us that much more is demanded than a mere rational grasp or mental assent: "A parable is 'performative'; it aims at and brings about an existential change." This effect is not peculiar to Jesus' parables, however, as some have claimed. His literal discourse (and others') can create the same performative effect—so too his actions (e.g., Lk 5:4–8; Jn 9:35–38). Nor is it primarily the form or technique of the parable that creates the effect, but the content—and the character of the teller.

APPLICATIONS TO JESUS' AUDIENCE

For a few parables the Gospels give no clear indication of the auspices in which Jesus was speaking. For many more the gospels' clear indications are often treated in modern scholarship as products of the evangelists or their sources, and not historically reliable. Scholars who theorize about Jesus' actual audiences try to match what they take to be the meaning of a parable with the most likely occasion for it in "the recorded experience of Jesus" (Cadoux, 55).

But we can gain little new knowledge about Jesus' meaning in a parable from this sort of theory about its original hearers, because it is based on someone's prior ideas about the meaning of the parable (Sider 1983).

The character, situation, and reactions of Jesus' audiences can direct interpretation. Unless we realize the Lost Son is Jesus' reply to criticism from the Pharisees, for instance, we can hardly decide what to make of the story's suspended conclusion. This sort of knowledge helps us with the Mustard Seed (Mk 4:30–32) and the Leaven (Mt 13:33).

INTERPRETIVE MODEL

Stein, 95

> The point of these parables then must be found in the contrast between the insignificant beginning of the kingdom of God and its final glory. Yet we can be even more specific than this. The main emphasis does not lie in the greatness of the kingdom of God in its final manifestation, for every Jew who heard Jesus would agree to this.... What was not recognized nor understood was the smallness and insignificance of its beginning. How differently and unexpectedly has the kingdom of God come. Rome is oblivious to its arrival, and even the Jewish leaders are blinded by their own religiosity. They cannot conceive that the wedding has begun and that such disreputable characters as the harlots, the publicans, the poor, the blind, are already now participating in the blessings of the kingdom. Although they have eyes, they do not see; although they have ears, they do not hear (MARK 4:12). For them the kingdom of God is hidden.

Since the tenor of the Mustard Seed and the Leaven is elliptical except for the general references to "the kingdom," Stein looks to the character and situation of Jesus' audience for cues. Matthew (13:34) says both parables are told to the crowd; therefore, Stein infers, Jesus' precise point is not likely to be something to which "every Jew who heard Jesus would agree" (e.g., "the greatness of the kingdom of God in its final manifestation"). Since many hearers— the leaders especially—are "blinded by their own religiosity" to the kingdom's small beginning, size is the aspect of the image that they need to hear.

Some parables, such as the Unjust Steward (Lk 16:1–13), elicited more than one reaction simultaneously from different audiences (Moessner, 159): "There is an audience change to the disciples in v. 1, though the Pharisees are still within earshot (v. 14)." We would assume that the disciples, as "people of the light" (v 8), took Jesus' admonition to heart as a word to the wisely meek. But the Pharisees' scoffing (v 14) suggests it is also his word to the foolishly proud; Jesus' rejoinder is a further cue (16:15): "You are the ones who justify yourselves in the eyes of men, but God knows your hearts."

Whenever we can imagine ourselves, even partly, in the situation of Jesus' audience his message is easily transferable from then to now. As Talbert says of the Lost Son (151), "Will the elder son accept the father's invitation to rejoice with him over the recovery of the prodigal as the shepherd's friends and the women's neighbors did with them? This is left open for each 'elder brother' who hears the parable to decide." The personal challenge, like the promise of Acts 2:39, "is for . . . all who are far off—for all whom the Lord our God will call."

EXERCISE

Exercises on the Two Debtors (Lk 7:41–47) and the Sower (Mk 4:3–8, 14–20)

1. Study the whole pericope of the Two Debtors for evidence about Jesus' audience of one, the Pharisee who entertained

him. How does it enrich Jesus' basic point that "He who has been forgiven little loves little" (v 47)?

2. Study the whole of Mark 4 for evidence about Jesus' two audiences here: "those on the outside" (v 11) and "the Twelve and the others around him" (v 10). What do their respective characters, situations, and reactions have to do with the meaning of the Sower?

See also Achtemeier on the Sower, and Resseguie (285–90) on the Two Debtors.

APPLICATIONS TO THE EVANGELISTS' READERS

How the gospel writers treat their materials frequently seems to reflect the situation of the early church more than Jesus' pre-resurrection audience. Matthew's version of the Lost Sheep, for example (18:12–14) occurs in a chapter that explicitly mentions the church (v 17); and his divergences from Luke's evangelistic version (15:3–7) suggest accommodation to the concerns of pastoral ministry—even though some such divergences may go back to Jesus himself, as Funk says (1966, 163 n.1): "Is it not likely that Jesus spoke a given parable on a number of occasions (this much is customarily granted) and in different contexts, adapting it each time, perhaps, to the circumstances?" (John Howard Yoder, lecture in his "Preface to Theology" course, Associated Biblical Seminaries, Elkhart, Fall 1971). Since every new company of hearers lives in a somewhat different situation, teachers and theologians in every age must decide what is "faithful change." The evangelists' adjustments of Jesus' message were one step.

The Great Supper (Lk 14:15–24), spoken as a warning to the unfaithful, is exploited in Luke as an exhortation to the faithful. Stein (90) notes the significance of this evangelist's additions. Unlike either Matthew or the Gospel of Thomas, he identifies the replacement guests as the poor, the maimed, the blind, and the lame (cf. Lk 4:18; 7:22; 14:13), in accord with his special theological concern for "the poor and the outcasts of the world." In addition, only Luke includes a second invitation to replacement guests: "Whereas the emphasis in the Matthean parable falls heaviest on the exclusion of those who rejected the invitation to the banquet, in Luke the emphasis falls more upon the inclusion of the outcasts in the banquet."

As Stein intimates, this kind of interpretation of Luke's alterations does not conflict with an evangelical doctrine of biblical inspiration. They are not a corruption of Jesus' purpose, but "an inspired application of this parable to the situation which Luke faced" (91). To find evidence of his editorial activity in his divergences from Matthew's parable of the Wedding Feast (Mt 22:1–14), Stein must assume that Luke's and Matthew's versions are variants of one parable of Jesus. They may actually be "different teachings of Jesus, using similar imagery, on two different occasions in his ministry" (Blomberg, 237), but we should emulate Stein's exemplary interpretive method.

Stein wants to identify Luke's application of the parable to the original audience of his gospel. The methods are twofold. (1) He compares Luke's version with the gospel parallels. An interpreter should collect all the identifiable divergences first; Stein comments on those that reflect Luke's special interest—the mention of the poor, maimed, blind, and lame, and the second quest for more guests. Rightly he implies that this evidence is stronger because these two features point in the same direction—to Luke's emphasis upon Jesus' concern for the poor and outcasts. (2) He compares Luke's distinctive touches with other parts of the gospel (Lk 4:18; 7:22; 14:13) that corroborate this interest, thus strengthening the conclusion that these divergences from Matthew and Thomas embody this theme, rather than some other. Stein then identifies the broader tendency of Luke's gospel that this theme embodies:

Luke has added an exhortation about charity to Jesus' eschatological warning.

Stein also wants to determine which details of the parable convey particular features of the theme. If we read Luke's parable by itself, without comparing Matthew and other parts of Luke, we might well hesitate to extend the theme beyond the terms which comprise the parable's fundamental analogies.

(1) God : Jewish leaders = host : guests originally invited with respect to retribution

(2) God : the dispossessed = host : participating guests with respect to gracious reception

But in the light of such comparisons, which highlight Luke's distinctive touches, we can feel confident about elaborating some of the details, and acknowledging God's gift of the gospel to the Gentiles.

outcasts of Israel = guests from streets and lanes

the Gentiles = guests from the highways and hedges

Thus Luke's extended application suggests a legitimate direction for our own.

Matthew too shows a concern to exhort his church audience (see Jeremias [43] on Going to Court, Mt 5:25–26); at times he also takes an interest in church politics. We know from Acts 6:1 (cf. Col 3:11) that the cross-cultural politics of Hebrew and Hellenized Jewish believers was a problem. The Jews' acceptance of Gentile believers was a bigger question still (e.g., Ac 10; 15:1–35; Gal 2–5); the issue of Jew and Gentile (Rom 9–11) affects Matthew's treatment of the Vineyard Laborers (Mt 20:1–16), as Drury observes (92–93).

Likewise Jesus' problem with the Pharisees' disdain of "sinners" (Lk 15:1–2) is analogous to, but not identical with, Luke's similar problem with the "Greco-Roman readers" that Talbert describes while defining "the Lukan view of the church" in the Physician for the Sick (Lk 5:30–32).

Talbert, 64

> [Jesus] indicates not only where he is to be found but also what credentials are required for his disciples: "The church is the only fellowship in the world where the one requirement for membership is the unworthiness of the candidate" (Robert Munger). Such an understanding of Jesus and his church was strange to Greco-Roman readers. In Origen's *Against Celsus*, 3:59f., Celsus, the pagan critic of Christianity, complains that ordinarily those invited to participate in religious solemnities are the pure who live an honorable life. Christians, however, invite anyone who is a sinner, or foolish, or simple-minded.... Origen does not deny the charge but says (3:60–61) Christians extend an invitation to sinners in order to bind up their wounds (id., 7:60).... If the Lukan Jesus is to be found in fellowship with sinners, the Lukan view of the church is that of a fellowship composed of social outcasts restored to community, and sinners forgiven by grace who have left all to follow Jesus.

Origen's apologetic shows that the problem persisted beyond the first century; that brings us to readers through the ages.

Exercise on the Lost Sheep (Mt 18:12–14; Lk 15:3–7)

To identify Matthew's intent for his first audience, construct the basic proportions that seem best suited to *each* version of this parable and study the fundamental divergences. Then list any further differences of detail. Matthew's special intent may be clearest where two or more differences point in the same direction or toward his special interests as manifested elsewhere, especially in chapter 18. Given his special concerns in the parable of the Lost Sheep, which details must be symbolic, and which may be?

See also Heil on the parables of Mark 4, and the discussion of various parables by Carlston, Donahue, and Gundry.

APPLICATIONS TO READERS THROUGH THE AGES

Every reader invests the biblical text with preconceived values and tends to ignore its other implications. The best corrective is the history of interpretation. Though we cannot perfectly construe what comes from another culture, or another community with its peculiar values and its shared associations with words, we may be able to use others' readings of the parables to break our narrow habits of thought when nothing else works. Talbert's reference to Origen (above) is one good example. If the gospel has made it a truism that God has "lifted up the humble" and "filled the hungry with good things" (Lk 1:52, 53), we need Origen's critics of Christianity to remind us that it has not always been so self-evident— and may not be today for every hearer of the gospel. Interpreters of past ages can be mind-stretching, even though we may be put off by some of their habits, such as the Schoolmen's "overly subtle or trivial reasoning" (Silva, 54). In our own time so much creative intelligence is exercised on the parables that it is hard to take full advantage of it.

Nevertheless Bailey's methods of "oriental exegesis" should encourage us to keep on looking, with as much imagination as possible, to avoid missing still other untapped possibilities (Bailey 1976, 29).

The culture that informs the text of the Gospel parables can be delineated in a relatively precise manner by bringing together three tools. The culture of contemporary conservative peasants must be examined to see what the parables mean in their setting. Oriental versions need to be studied to see how Oriental churchmen through the centuries have translated the text. Ancient literature pertinent to the parables must be read *with* the insights gained from these other two sources, not in isolation from them.

His first two tools are unconventional but intriguing examples of particular interpretive groups whose responses we should seek out. Oriental translators of the Bible are seldom cited as interpreters of the parables. And in studying "the culture of contemporary conservative peasants" Bailey has improved greatly upon the conventional methods, which he calls "the view from the saddle," "the view from the study window," and "the view from the single village" (32). His twenty years with a literacy team as "an ordinary resident" in "the most isolated and primitive" oriental villages gave him access to "a wide range of village people and village pastors" in "a relationship of intimacy and trust that has made possible the asking of cultural questions related to the parables" (35). The results, he says, "in some cases confirm what we already know." But "other known insights are refined, still others rejected, and some new raw material has been uncovered to aid in parabolic understanding" (36). It is hard to imagine discovering another new enterprise of special research on the parables that would be as intriguing as this one. But we should exercise our creative intelligence in the hope of finding more such means of illuminating the parables.

As scholars keep stimulating one another's thinking, so students should seek to be stimulated. Talbert (156) says that Ellis worked out the relation of the Unjust Steward to the context that follows it in Luke (16:14ff.) by "following a hint by John Calvin." Likewise in Drury's "amplification" (82–84) of Kingsbury on Matthew 13, one interpreter picks up where the other leaves off.

See also Ireland (305–7). We may be equally moved to articulateness by our disagreements with others. Human nature being what it is, perhaps no models are necessary for that.

EXERCISE

Exercises on Selected Parables

1. Choose an interpretation in this book that has especially stimulated your thinking. Find a way to either (a) build on its ideas about the parable(s) already under discussion, or (b) apply the method to some other parable(s).
2. Choose an interpretation with which you strongly disagree. Write a rebuttal that marshals and focuses your own perceptions and judgments about how the parable works and what Jesus means.

SUMMARY OF PART 3

1. Any external feature of a parable may be crucial to its meaning, especially as a cue to the extent and limits of the allegorical symbolism.
2. To determine how the meaning of a parable is defined by the *acculturation* reflected in Jesus' stories and audience, interpreters need special knowledge of life in ancient Palestine, and of Jewish theology, history, folklore, and symbols.
3. Hearing a parable of Jesus as his hearers heard it requires knowledge of their expectations about this particular *genre* of analogy in image or story—as reflected in analogues from the Old Testament, from rabbinic and early Christian teaching, and even from the literature of Greece, Rome, and other traditions.

4. A parable of Jesus does not achieve its whole meaning in isolation, but only in the *literary context* of Jesus' other teachings, the evangelists' purposes in their Gospels, and the rest of the Bible.

5. There are substantial benefits to be gained from the experience of other interpreters of the parables, in the time of Jesus and the early church, and in every age since.

Conclusion: Synthesis

When we simply read the parables we can respond spontaneously and subtly to many of its features all at one time, but only selectively and imperfectly. That is why when we carefully study them we try to refine those responses by reflection and to fill in the gaps—but not all of them at once. The *analysis* in parts 1, 2, and 3 is a necessary labor of considering each feature of a parable separately. We merely "murder to dissect" if we stop here though, and do not recover again the impact of the whole parable, not as we found it on the first reading, but in a newly informed *synthesis*. Putting it all together should be the aim of any interpretive essay. Such a synthesis will give most space and emphasis to the interpretive topics that are most important for the individual parable, arranging them in logical or climactic order; on other aspects it will touch more briefly or not at all. It should, however, address a large and diverse number of interpretive considerations. An excellent model of this synthesizing process is Blomberg's interpretation (233–37) of the Great Supper (Lk 14:15–24), which brings to bear on the parable a judicious and generous selection of the topics covered in this book, including grammar, plot structure, narrative details, Palestinian culture, traditional stories, the parable's contexts (episode, chapter, Old Testament), and others' interpretations.

DELIMITING ALLEGORY

One fact emerging from part 2 is that any feature of a parable may convey a point, even the main point. That is the most important reason for attempting all the trial-formulas for proportional analogy that one can conceive for a parable before trying to discern which particular analogies express Jesus' message. But not all features of a parable are allegorical symbols; some details are purely literal furnishings of plot, character, and other features of a story. How can we tell the difference?

We can look to secular practical criticism for some indication of "how to determine which and how many details in a given parable 'stand for' something or someone other than themselves" as Blomberg suggests (48), but there we will find that the sufficient rules are never simple and seldom clearly articulated. Most interpreters of allegorical authors such as Dante, Spenser, Bunyan, and Orwell do not tell how to identify the symbols; they just do it. Their practice reflects the free operation of highly experienced critical instincts—a grace that lies beyond the reach of rules. The parables require a similar enterprise. Yet certain criteria for distinguishing symbols reappear regularly in secular interpretive practice, and these can help us to a point. Most criteria, taken singly, establish only some degree of likelihood; they are more helpful where two or more agree together.

The more prominent or central a story feature is, the more likely it is to be symbolic. Conversely, the more marginal the detail, the less the likelihood, other things being equal. This is a criterion of *proportion*. Hence the reasoning that the second half of the Lost Son—the elder brother's episode—must make a point of its own; if the only point had to do with the prodigal, Jesus would have ended with his welcome-home. Even Jeremias, a staunch believer in the one-point theory, calls this parable "double-edged" (131).

We may need a good reason for *not* taking some feature of a parable symbolically, if the doctrine involved is paralleled in Jesus' own teaching. Perrin has proposed a "criterion of *dis*similarity" for quite a different purpose: determining which sayings in the Gospels cannot possibly be regarded as subsequent additions to

Jesus' actual words, because they are like nothing anyone but Jesus was saying (Perrin 1971, 39–43). The criterion of *similarity* supports symbolic possibilities that cannot easily be denied to Jesus because they are so characteristic. The prodigal's shoes may not be the "preparation of the gospel of peace," but his repentance symbolizes the sincerity that Jesus wants the Pharisees to see in the "sinners" who gathered to hear him (Lk 15:1–2). This criterion also can be used negatively, where a potential symbolic meaning is too much at odds with Jesus' teaching. Thus Bailey, on the Barren Fig Tree (Lk 13:6–9), appeals both to Jesus' doctrine and to common Jewish belief (1980, 84–85):

> The vinedresser has often been identified with Jesus, who is then seen arguing with God the Father. Such an identification could hardly have been imagined by the original audience nor intended by Jesus. The Christian allegorizer begins with his theology of the Trinity and from that makes the above identification. But when he does so, God the Father is seen as harsh and judgmental, and Jesus appears as gracious and loving.

Jülicher could have refuted much of the old tradition of incongruous allegorizing simply by invoking this criterion of similarity.

A symbolic meaning might fit Jesus' teaching but not a particular occasion. Blomberg (234) applies a criterion of *relevance* to the Great Supper: "It is just possible that the excuses for participating in a Jewish holy war are in view (Deut 20:5–9), in which case the point would be one of contrast—legitimate excuses against serving in the Israelite army no longer apply to the call to enlist in God's 'kingdom troops.'" Blomberg's hesitation probably has to do with the question of this topic's relevance for Jesus' response to the Pharisee's guest (Lk 14:15). Conversely, the more relevance a potential symbolic meaning has for the immediate situation, the greater the likelihood that it is no mere coincidence. For example, Jeremias limits the Sower to one point: the contrast of an allegedly bleak prospect and the eventual "harvest of reward beyond all asking or conceiving" (150). But if he appreciated the urgent relevance of the unfruitful soils to Mark's story of people who neither understand the parables (4:11–12; cf. v 9) nor join "the others around him" with the Twelve (4:10) in requesting an explanation, he would have one less reason to reject the gospel explanation of the parable as a secondary addition to Jesus' parabolic image.

Not every part of a parable has symbolic meaning. Servants are required to make the plot of the Great Supper work; this is a sufficient explanation for their presence. To invoke the criterion of *indispensability* we need to ask: Is this particular symbolism essential to Jesus' main point? Thus to be understood Jesus' reply to the Pharisees in the Lost Son (Lk 15:11–32) does not require a symbolic reading of the prodigal's ring, robe, and shoes.

Conversely, this criterion may support a symbolic reading. Blomberg argues that the implausibility of so many simultaneously rejected invitations in the Great Supper "suggests an allegorical level" (234). This explanation is indispensable if the probable social dynamics of the time provide none. Thus implausibilities are one sort of feature that ought to be taken as potentially symbolic (cf. Huffman). A second sort are seemingly superfluous details, as in the Two Builders (Mt 7:24–27).

INTERPRETIVE MODEL

Gundry, 134–35

> Matthew . . . has great interest in the impregnability of the house on the rock. This corresponds to the impregnability of the church on the rock (see 16:18 again). To dramatize that impregnability, he details a storm instead of contenting himself with a passing reference to a flooding river (so the tradition, reflected by Luke). Just as in Luke the three details of digging, going deep,

and laying a foundation follow a general statement about building, Matthew works up to a general statement about the testing of the house with the three details of rain, rivers, and winds. There is no rain or winds in Luke, but only an overflowing river near the house. In Matthew a cloud bursts, flash floods race down the usually dry ravines—hence the plural of rivers in place of Luke's singular—and winds blow fiercely during the storm. A statement that the house did not fall climaxes Matthew's impressive list of parallel statements beginning with καί. . . .

[In the second half of the parable] "ground" gives way to "sand." Matthew has switched from a flooding river to a cloudburst and here has in mind loose soil washed down by previous flash floods into a concourse of steep ravines. The stupidity of building there exceeds even the stupidity of building without a foundation on a riverbank. And the alluvial sand makes an even more striking picture of instability, contrasting with the impregnability of the house on the rock.

To make such systematic alterations in the tradition he has received, Matthew surely must have a symbolic point.

The *coherence of the analogy* is another way of applying positively the criterion of indispensability. Once we are certain that the Great Supper (Lk 14:15–24) is symbolic of "the end-time celebration of God's people" (Blomberg, 233) we know what persons are symbolized by the host and the guests. These additional symbols are indispensable because the logic of the analogy forces them on us. The relationship of God to the end-time celebration tells us that the host must be God if the banquet symbolizes the end-time celebration. Likewise in the parable of the Tenants (Mk 12:1–12), once we recognize Israel in the image of the vineyard, we know who the owner, tenants, and servants must be.

ASKING THE RIGHT QUESTIONS

There is much more to interpreting a parable than drawing the line on allegory—so much more that it might seem that the thorough interpreter should give attention to every conceivable aspect of a parable and method of interpretation. There are, however, at least two limiting factors. For one thing, different people's minds work best by different means. Just as certain authors' literary works may repel us, so some interpretive methods may not suit our natural or acquirable gifts. We may grow as interpreters by seriously trying some things that come hard at first; but we should have an eye for diminishing returns. One will always deal best with certain questions. Secondly, different parables work by different means. The aspects (and the answerable methods) that are most crucial for one parable may be marginal in another. Each parable is a new problem, and every new problem dictates its own questions—if we have ears to hear.

Asking the right questions is one of the most valuable initiatives of independent thought that one can bring to any productive human endeavor—from leadership and problem-solving to the arts, technology, and science—not excluding interpretation of the parables. Often it is much harder to find the right question than to answer it. This book broaches many questions; as a precedent to inventing more, one may consider the good example of Stein (106) at work on the Unjust Steward (Lk 16:1–8).

> In seeking to understand the point of this notoriously difficult parable, the interpreter encounters a number of serious problems. Stated simply they are:
> 1. Where does the parable end?
> 2. Why was the steward called "dishonest"?
> 3. Is the behavior of the master conceivable?
> 4. To what kind of audience did Jesus address this parable?

How did Stein generate these questions? He found the first one ready-made, for interpreters have argued long about that. The rest have been asked before also; chances are that his thinking is not a model of inventing original questions, but rather of something else equally important (and sometimes very difficult): identifying the truly important questions from among all those being asked.

We can hardly make rules for this process, but it can help to imagine how it might have worked for Stein. He must have answered each of these four questions before he decided that "the key to Jesus' thinking" (110) must be the commendation of the steward's prudence (Lk 16:8).

INTERPRETIVE MODEL

Stein, 111

> The man in our parable had the cunning cleverness to prepare for the judgment awaiting him from his master. . . . Jesus by this parable urges his audience to be prudent also. . . .
>
> Luke in his redaction takes this point of Jesus and applies it to his audience. . . . Since the parable involves bills, debts, money, Luke appends to the parable various sayings of Jesus dealing with money in vs. 9–13 and one that urges the followers of Jesus to act prudently with regard to their own material well-being.

Perhaps Stein tentatively reached these conclusions very early in his thinking about the parable, by the kind of intuition that goes with spontaneous reading. If so, to test his hypothesis he needed to answer these four questions. Or he might have begun with an intuition that these are important questions and let the answers lead him to his conclusions.

Like problem-solving and other intensely creative activities, generating interpretive questions and recognizing the good ones is a very untidy mental process, partly rational and partly intuitive, and very hard to teach except by trial and error. Intelligence is necessary but not sufficient; there is no substitute for hard work (restless, resourceful, sustained concentration), reflection (just "sleeping on it"), and experience (the more you do it, the better you get).

One way to focus the question-*choosing* process for a particular parable is to ask: Of all the topics and methods in this book, which embody the most important questions? The only way to be sure, of course, is to experiment by applying questions, whether they look promising or not. While framing the exercises in this book I was quite often surprised at the insights that emerged from the seemingly mechanical process of matching questions with parables. To focus the question-*generating* process it helps to ask: What are the most striking, emphatic, unusual, surprising, mysterious, or just intriguing features of this parable? Another question is just as important: What topics *not* covered in this book are important for this parable?

Adopting others' questions has the efficiency of standing on others' shoulders, but it has some of the drawbacks of too much reverence for the authority of precedent. Can we detect people's tacit assumptions in their questions? Can we recognize fallacious assumptions? We should not shrink from reflecting on even the most apparently silly or wrong-headed questions; articulating our objections often leads to new questions, or even some good use for the original one.

Where should the questions begin? What comes first to one's mind about a parable? Almost anything can, depending on the parable and the reader. Since a good hypothesis may be inspired by any aspect of a parable, it is too inhibiting to lay down a rule like Quentin Quesnell's (as described by Donfried, 428), "that one always begin with the smallest circle, the text or pericope under discussion, and that one only move to the next step, the larger circle, as the previous one ceases to yield information for an adequate exegesis." This may suit Donfried's search for the significance of the Ten Maidens' oil (Mt 25:1–13), but it is not a good plan for the Tenants (Mk 12:1–12), where the vineyard—from the outermost circle, the Old Testament—is fundamental to everything else.

It would not always be a good plan, either, to start with the smallest linguistic units, moving on to larger and larger units, both rhetorical and narrative, and leaving external features of the parable for last, as we have done in parts 2 and 3. In some cases we might need word studies as a preliminary to analyzing parallelisms, plotting, or dialogue, but in others we might need experience with any of those features just to know which words need special study. It is best to start with what appears most striking, and later to reassess, in the light of later discoveries, your judgments about your first considerations.

REACHING CONCLUSIONS

A good interpretation can begin anywhere, but eventually, by whatever route, it must be made as thorough and systematic as one's talents and time permit. The final outcome of the interpreter's process of reflection must, of course, be orderly and coherent. But any comprehensive guidelines that begin with "Take these interpretive steps in the following order" will inhibit the interpreter's originality of thought in classification, analysis, synthesis, and evaluation—mental activities which, at the beginning of the process of interpretation, can be more fruitful and productive in direct proportion as they are more spontaneous, unpredictable—and inevitably messy. The more questions we ask (and the more diverse) the better our work, if we succeed in integrating the answers well. The challenge is to recognize as many potential cues to meaning as we possibly can.

This enterprise should bring us closer to discovering the truth, the whole truth, and nothing but the truth about a parable, but obviously there are no guarantees. Some cues suggest one message; others generate divergent or contradictory ideas. Which deserve the most weight? Different readers, with their own beliefs, habits of mind, and preoccupations, will find virtually limitless combinations of significant cues and endless ways of weighting their relative importance. Is it any wonder that interpreters of the parables, like readers of other literature, disagree endlessly? Though we should strive for objectivity of interpretation, we can never fully achieve it. "Now we know in part." We do what we can. But whenever interpreters read the parables again, they never know what new response may spark a genuine discovery.

Appendix A

JÜLICHER ON LITERAL AND FIGURATIVE IN THE PARABLES

Jülicher's determination to banish allegory from the parables leads him to deny any figurative element in the parables, reinforcing his arbitrary distinction between parable and allegory with another artificial distinction. Though our common experience of reading shows that almost all metaphors are instantly intelligible, he says that because metaphor "does not mean what it says" it hides its meaning while simile is transparent, "meaning what it says" (author's translation, here and below).

He denies any blending or exchange of the two (I, 52–53), despite the fact that the transition from simile (e.g., Mt 25:32) to metaphor (25:33) can be spontaneous and unobtrusive. Considering metaphor to be figurative speech and simile to be literal, he defines allegory as extended metaphor, i.e., strictly figurative, and parable as extended simile, i.e., strictly literal (I, 58). Therefore the antithesis between parable and allegory "admits no mingling of kinds" (76).

The singular result is that Jülicher treats all parables not as *figurative* comparisons but as *literal* examples; the Unworthy Servants, for instance (Lk 17:7–10), is a literal instance of a general rule about servants and masters. For him the genuinely literal "example-stories"—the Good Samaritan (Lk 10:25–37), the Rich Fool (Lk 12:13–21), the Rich Man and Lazarus (Lk 16:19–31), and the Pharisee and Publican (Lk 18:9–14)—are distinct from the rest of Jesus' parables merely because they require no transfer from another sphere to the spiritual (I, 112).

This is a fact not yet well enough known. For though Jülicher calls the parables "literal" in his English-language article, "Parable," in *Encyclopedia Biblica* (1902), English-speaking scholars who know him chiefly from his German work, *Die Gleichnisreden Jesu* (1888, 1899), have misunderstood the crucial word *uneigentlich*. When Jülicher calls parables *eigentlich* he means "literal"; when he calls allegory *uneigentlich* he means "figurative" (e.g., I, 49, 73), which is a normal German usage. He also uses *uneigentlich* interchangeably with *metaphorische* (e.g., I, 55, 63).

But from Browne (1913, 35) to Tolbert (1979, 27–28) English-speaking scholars have read his *uneigentlich* as "inauthentic" and *eigentlich* (when applied to parable) as "authentic." (For "figurative" they may be expecting *bildlich*.) Various paradoxes have resulted. Browne thinks *eigentlich* denotes a branch of the figurative; Via applies *uneigentlich* to allegory but not, with Jülicher, to metaphor. Smith (18) and Perrin (1967, 257) endorse Jülicher's view of the parables as *eigentlich* while asserting their figurative qualities. Tolbert (27) says *metaphor* was "a pejorative term for Jülicher," though in fact he speaks approvingly (I, 55) of Jesus' use of metaphor such as the Leaven of the Pharisees (Lk 12:1); it is allegory (= extended metaphor) that he deprecates.

Why this confusion? English speakers, not supposing that Jülicher could so oddly deny figurative language in the parables, have taken "inauthentic" to denote the obscurity of allegory (so Via, 7–8, Tolbert, 1979, 27). German scholars have understood him, but without showing much interest; Kümmel (186) says Jülicher "goes too far," but does not pursue the implications.

It was not Jülicher's intent with the word *uneigentlich* to call allegory inauthentic, but rather to deny any figurative comparison in the *story-parables* (analogies elaborated to story length and complexity, such as the Lost Son, Lk 15:11–32). He did this both by associating story-parables exclusively with literal language, and by neglecting to acknowledge the form of the proportional analogy anywhere but in the simplest *similitudes* (parables of less than story length and complexity, such as the Asking Son, Mt 7:9–11), thus restricting Jesus' figurative language to simple *metaphors* (such as calling Herod "that fox"—Lk 13:32). The implications of this theory for Jülicher's practice of interpreting parables have been commonly recognized, if not traced to their cause (e.g., Jeremias 19):

> The broadest application will prove to be the true one. "The story of the rich man and poor Lazarus was intended to induce joy in a life of suffering, and fear of the life of pleasure" (Luke 16.19–31). That "even the richest of men is at every moment wholly dependent upon the power and mercy of God" is the lesson of the parable of the Rich Fool (Luke 12.16ff.). "Wise use of the present as the condition of a happy future" is the lesson of the parable of the Unjust Steward (Luke 16.1–8). The original form of Matt. 24.45–51 was intended to stir up the disciples to "the most earnest fulfilment of their duty toward God." "A reward is only earned by performance" is the fundamental idea of the parable of the Talents (Matt. 25.14ff.).

Jeremias notes that such generalized truths suited Jülicher's understanding of Jesus as "a teacher of wisdom who inculcates moral precepts" rather than an eschatological preacher, but he does not link the outcome of Jülicher's interpretation with his curious theory that the parables are purely literal speech.

It is possible that few interpreters, or none at all, have closely emulated Jülicher's interpretation of all the parables as literal example-stories until Via, whose existential concerns also are accommodated by understanding each parable as invoking a particular example for the sake of a general truth. Via reads the parables as literal examples, not as figurative analogies. He too makes the broadest application: "God gives to the man who has nothing a place to exist meaningfully before himself . . . without regard for human considerations of merit" (the Vineyard Laborers, 155); "the present is a crisis because the future is threatening, and . . . man by making an appropriate response to the crisis can overcome the danger" (the Unjust Steward, 161); "natural man does not know God as the one who forgives radically and does not know himself as accepted in spite of his unacceptability" (the Lost Son, 173).

Appendix B

OLD TESTAMENT ANALOGUES TO THE PARABLES OF JESUS

In addition to the examples cited in the sections on Old Testament *meshalim* and story-parables, the following texts are significant precedents for Jesus' parables.

1. DESCRIPTIONS AND HYPOTHETICAL INSTANCES

Splintered Reed (2Ki 18:21; Is 36:6); Donkey, Ox, Unsalted Food, and Egg White (Job 6:4–7); Papyrus (Job 8:11–13); Washing with Soap (Job 9:30–31); the Felled Tree (Job 14:7–10); Besieger (Job 19:12); Looking at the Sun (Job 37:21–24); Ant (Prov 6:6–8); Wind and Womb (Eccl 11:4–5); Ravaged Body (Is 1:5–6); Egg Stealers (Is 10:14); Ax, Saw, Rod, and Club (Is 10:15); Ripe Fig (Is 28:4); Broken Wall and Pottery (Is 30:12–14); Vine Gone Wild (Jer 2:21); Destroyed Tent (Jer 10:20); Ethiopian and Leopard (Jer 13:23); Grape Pickers and Thieves (Jer 49:9–10; Obad 5–6); Bear and Snake (Amos 5:18–19); Soaring Eagle (Obad 2–4); Defilement (Hag 2:11–14).

Cf. the Two Masters (Mt 6:24); the Empty House (Mt 12:43–45); Clean and Unclean (Mt 15:10–20); the Patched Garment and the Wineskins (Mk 2:21–22); the Asking Son (Lk 11:11–13); Places at Table (Lk 14:7–11); the Lost Sheep and Coin (Lk 15:3–10).

2. Sustained Narratives

Undependable Streams (Job 6:15–21); Well-Watered Plant (Job 8:16–19); Mine (Job 28:1–28); Wanton Queen (Is 47:5–15); Marauding Army (Joel 2:1–11); Butchers (Mic 3:1–3).

Cf. the Hidden Treasure (Mt 13:44); the Pearl (Mt 13:45–46); the Net (Mt 13:47–50); the Two Sons (Mt 21:28–32); the Two Debtors (Lk 7:41–47); the Barren Fig Tree (Lk 13:6–9).

3. Mixed Literal and Figurative Discourse

Tree by Water (Ps 1:3); Woman in Labor (Is 26:17–18); Cornerstone in Zion (Is 28:16–17); Treader of the Winepress (Is 63:1–6); Sudden Birth (Is 66:7–11); Harlot Wife (Jer 3:1–25); Thriving Olive (Jer 11:16–17); Scattering Shepherds (Jer 23:1–14); Prodigal Daughter (Ezek 16); Oholah and Oholibah (Ezek 23); Cooking Pot (Ezek 24).

Cf. Salt of the Earth (Mt 5:13); Light of the World (Mt 5:14–16); the Door (Jn 10:1–10); the Good Shepherd (Jn 10:11–18); the Vine and Branches (Jn 15:5–8).

The Old Testament also contains special kinds of parabolic expression not represented in the Gospels. There are *eyewitness reports:* the Potter's House (Jer 18:1ff.) and the Recabites' Vow (Jer 35:1ff.), both with the prophet's "interpretation." This kind of symbolism takes us a step in the direction of *object-lesson symbols* like Jeremiah's basket of figs (24) and Ezekiel's sticks (37:15ff.), or the prophets' *parabolic actions,* a special sort of symbol that does have parallels in Jesus' ministry (Jeremias 227–29). And there are symbolic *dreams* and *visions:* Joseph's (Gen 37:5–9), Pharaoh's (Gen 41:17–32), his butler's and baker's (Gen 40:4–18), Ezekiel's (chap. 37), Nebuchadnezzar's (Dan 2:31–45), and Daniel's (chaps. 7, 8, 10–12). Peter's Sheet of Unclean Animals (Acts 10:11–16) and the apocalyptic visions of the Revelation are New Testament parallels.

GLOSSARY

Cross-referenced terms are marked with SMALL CAPITALS.

Allegory. In strict usage, a device of RHETORIC consisting of ANALOGY extended from one PROPORTION, POINT OF RESEMBLANCE, or SYMBOL to two or more (e.g., Shakespeare's *Hamlet* 1.4.23–38: the Vicious Mole; and Lk 12:35–40: the Waiting Servants); in loose usage, a literary work in which this rhetorical device is sustained and pervasive (e.g., Bunyan's *Pilgrim's Progress;* and Mk 12:1–12: the Tenants), not just intermittent or incidental (e.g., Donne's "Valediction: Forbidding Mourning"; and Mt 5–7: the Sermon on the Mount). Allegory is found in many literary works of all sorts, including DISCOURSE, NARRATIVE, drama, and lyric verse. Almost all of Jesus' parables are allegories in the loose sense, because the comparison is elaborated beyond a single proportional analogy, point of resemblance, or symbol.

Contrary to the categorical statements of many New Testament scholars, allegories vary greatly with respect to their literary form, their unrealism, and the extent of their symbolism. Some allegories are pictorial descriptions (e.g., Portia's image of the dying swan in Shakespeare's *Merchant of Venice,* 3.2.43–47; and Mk 2:16–17: the Physician for the Sick); some are hypothetical instances (e.g., 1Cor 12:12–27: The Body of Christ; and Mt 18:12–14: the Lost Sheep); and many are narratives (e.g., Menenius' FABLE of the Belly in Shakespeare's *Coriolanus,* 1.1.96ff.; and Lk 15:11–32: the Lost Son). Some allegories have images that are implausible or fantastic (e.g., Ezek 17:3–24: the Cedar, Eagle, and Vine), but other allegorical images are entirely or essentially lifelike (e.g., Aesop's fable of the volatile sailors, the Watchman of Ezek 33:2–9, and all of Jesus' allegorical parables). In a few literary works (such as Tasso's *Gerusalemme Liberata*) the allegorical symbolism seems to be pervasive; that is, every detail has symbolic meaning. But in most allegorical works, including Spenser's *Faerie Queene,* Bunyan's *Pilgrim's*

Progress, Orwell's *Animal Farm,* and parables of Jesus such as the Weeds (Mt 13:24–30, 37–43), the symbolism is selective; that is, many details have symbolic meaning, but some are purely literal embellishments of the plot, characters, and setting.

Allusion. The RHETORICAL device of reminding an audience of some prior knowledge or experience, used to enrich the language of a literary work with the whole range of the audience's ready-made associations with a familiar idea. Jesus' parables, for example, include many literary allusions to the Old Testament, such as the reminder in the Tenants (Mk 12:1) of Isaiah's Song of the Vineyard (Is 5:1–7).

Analogy. A verbal comparison that combines a TENOR, a VEHICLE, and one or more POINTS OF RESEMBLANCE in a structure of logic specially suited to serve as illustration or argument. Almost all of Jesus' parables are analogies of equation, but a few are analogies of example (see EXAMPLE-STORY), and a few are in part analogies of CLASSIFICATION. In Jesus' analogies of equation the language sometimes embodies SIMILE and sometimes METAPHOR, but always the structure is *proportional analogy,* logically equivalent to the mathematical proportion A : B = a : b (e.g., Shakespeare's *King Lear,* 4.1.37: "As flies to wanton boys are we to the gods"). Rarely does a parable of Jesus involve only one proportional analogy; usually his meaning depends on two or more, and this extension or elaboration of simple analogy creates ALLEGORY.

Archetype. A literary SYMBOL that gains special force of idea and emotion from its connection with experiences universal to humanity, such as life and death and the cycle of the seasons (e.g., Mk 13:28–29: the Budding Fig Tree).

Byword. A particular person, nation, etc. treated as a parable, especially a horrifying EXAMPLE, either of divine judgment on one's evil ways (e.g., Dt 28:37; and Lk 12:13–21: the Rich Fool), or the troubles that come unjustly to the righteous (e.g., Ps 69:11).

Characterization. The portrayal of the traits and personality of a character in a literary work, either by direct description (e.g., Mt 25:26: "You wicked, lazy servant!") or by the implications of the character's behavior (25:18: "But the man ... hid his master's money"), of other characters' responses (25:28: "Throw that worthless servant outside"), or of a *character foil*—a different sort of personality whose presence emphasizes the character's traits through contrast (25:17: "The one with the two talents gained two more").

Chiasmus. A RHETORICAL device of inverted PARALLELISM, in which one pair of parallel elements envelops another pair in the order A B B A. One rhetorical potential of this device is to give the idea conveyed by the A-pair the double prominence of first place and END STRESS, e.g., Jn 1:10:

> *He* was in the *world*, and the *world* was made through *him*.
> A   B   A   B

Classification. A mode of ANALOGY in which the TENOR is a particular instance or example of the general category that constitutes the VEHICLE. This mode is different both from (1) analogy of example (see EXAMPLE-STORY), which has the opposite relation of tenor and vehicle, and from (2) analogy of equation (comprising the bulk of Jesus' PARABLES), in which both tenor and vehicle are particular examples of a general class that is stated or implied. None of Jesus' parables is mainly an analogy of classification, but in a few cases some features of his meaning are conveyed by this mode of logic. For further explanation and examples see Sider, 1981.

Climax. In any plotted NARRATIVE, including PARABLE, a high point of emotional excitement. Usually the principal climax of a narrative directly precedes the RESOLUTION.

Comedy. A kind of drama (or in broader use, of NARRATIVE, e.g., Dante's *Divine Comedy*) in which the principal characters' enterprise is threatened or impeded by complications of the plot (especially conflicts among themselves), and brought nevertheless to a successful end that is marked by new or renewed social unity, such as marriage or reconciliation of family or friends. Though pervasive humor is often regarded as an invariable feature of comedy, the term *comic* can refer specifically to this plot pattern of a threatened enterprise brought to success (contrast TRAGEDY)—as in some parables, e.g., the Hidden Treasure (Mt 13:44), the Lost Sheep and Coin (Lk 15:3–10), and the Unjust Judge (Lk 18:1–8). Because Jesus' message concerns the significance of accepting or rejecting God's commands, more parables are *tragicomic*—that is, the ending is happy for some and unhappy for others, e.g., the Two Builders (Mt 7:24–27), the Two Sons (Mt 21:28–32), the Two Ways (Mt 7:13–14), the Two Debtors (Lk 7:41–47), the Ten Maidens (Mt 25:1–13), the Talents (Mt 25:14–30), the Sheep and Goats (Mt 25:31–46), the Great Supper (Lk 14:15–24).

Connotation. The emotional or otherwise personal associations that an audience spontaneously attaches to language because of prior experience with particular words. This subjective content of a word or phrase is to be distinguished from DENOTATION, the more rational and objective element in the content of a word.

Denotation. The rational and objective content of language, as distinct from CONNOTATION—the emotional and personal content that individuals or groups associate with particular words and phrases. For example, the denotation of the word *Samaritan* is a designation of religious, ethnic, and geographic origin; but for Jews of Jesus' time the connotations included the idea of "despised archenemy" (Lk 10:33).

Denouement. See Resolution.

Diction. A speaker or writer's choice of individual words.

Discourse. Verbal expression in any mode, such as NARRATIVE or drama; in a narrower sense (somewhat confusingly), certain closely allied modes of discourse including essay, public speech, and private talk, as distinct from narrative and drama. In this sense the word *discourse* distinguishes Jesus' preaching and teaching in general from the narrative mode to which he often resorts in the parables. When his preaching includes a succession of SIMILITUDES—i.e., nonnarrative "discourse" in this narrower sense—we may call the series a *discursive sequence* of parables, e.g., most of Matthew 7.

Doublet. A pair of parables juxtaposed because of their common pertinence to a single theme of Jesus, e.g., the Tower Builder and the Warring King (Lk 14:26–33). *Triplets* include the Patched Garment, the Wineskins, and the Old and New Wine (Lk 5:36–39), and the Lost Sheep, Coin, and Son (Lk 15:1–32).

Ellipsis. The RHETORICAL device of omitting certain words, events, or ideas which are left for the audience to infer. Most of Jesus' parables are *elliptical,* omitting explicit mention of the ANALOGY's SIGNAL OF COMPARISON, POINT(S) OF RESEMBLANCE, and/or TENOR, or even part of the VEHICLE. The parable of the Tenants (Mt 21:33–46) involves ellipsis in all of these respects.

End Stress. The RHETORICAL device of emphasizing a word, event, person, place, or thing at the end of a series, which is the position of psychological CLIMAX, i.e., the position of greatest prominence in an audience's expectations. For example, in Jesus' parable the arrival and identity of the Samaritan derives special emphasis from his position at the end of a series of passersby, after the priest and Levite (Lk 10:31–33).

Equation. See ANALOGY.

Example-Story. A NARRATIVE ANALOGY of example, to be distinguished from the story-parable because its VEHICLE is a particular instance or example of the general category that constitutes the TENOR. For example, the Good Samaritan (Lk 10:25–37) is a single example used by Jesus to characterize the category of all good neighbors. Three other parables commonly acknowledged to be example-stories are the Rich Fool (Lk 12:13–21), the Rich Man and Lazarus (Lk 16:19–31), and the Pharisee and the Publican (Lk 18:9–14). The Places at Table (Lk 14:7–11) also is best understood in this mode.

Fable. A term denoting STORY-PARABLE, but sometimes including features not represented in Jesus' parables, such as the talking and racing animals in the "Hare and the Tortoise." Orwell's *Animal Farm* is a beast-fable elaborated to the length of a novel.

Genre. A species or kind of literature, sometimes identified mainly by form (e.g., ANALOGY), sometimes mainly by content (e.g., TAUNT), and sometimes by both (e.g., TRAGEDY, which is dramatic in form and catastrophic in content).

Hyperbole. The RHETORICAL device of overstatement or exaggeration for emphasis.

Image. Verbal description and/or narration concerning physical objects and settings, or characters, events, or other concrete and particular subjects. In this literary sense *image* denotes all the VEHICLES of Jesus' parables, whether purely descriptive (e.g., Mt 23:27–28: Whitewashed Sepulchers) or hypothetical (e.g., Lk 11:11–13: the Asking Son), or NARRATIVE (e.g., Lk 16:1–8: the Unjust Steward).

Irony. A RHETORICAL effect created by language or situation which the audience perceives to be incongruous with its context, e.g., the Unmerciful Servant's impossible promise: "Be patient with me . . . and I will pay back everything" (Mt 18:26).

Mashal. A Hebrew word denoting "likeness" generally, applied to various forms of comparison in ANALOGY, both of equation and example, as well as in RIDDLE, PROVERB, TAUNT, and BYWORD. Apparently the meaning of the term was subsequently generalized—first to include instances of proverbs, and such special types, that were not analogies; and later to include still more figures of speech and almost any special use of language, such as *poem* (Nu 21:27), *oration* (Job 27:1), *discourse* or *oracle* (Nu 24:15), and *wisdom* (Pr 1:6). Thus the term *mashal* comprises everything denoted by the evangelists' usage of *parabole* as PARABLE, and a great deal more.

Meiosis. The RHETORICAL device of understatement for subtle emphasis.

Metaphor. An ANALOGY of equation in which the presence of a comparison is only implied, rather than (as in SIMILE) expressed directly by *like, as,* or some similar SIGNAL OF COMPARISON. Whereas the explicit comparison of a simile can make its point in purely *literal* language, most metaphors are *figurative* language because a word denoting the VEHICLE is figuratively substituted for a word that would denote the TENOR literally (e.g., Jn 4:34: "My *food* is to do the will of him who sent me, and to accomplish his work"). Occasionally, however, the comparison of an analogy is implied without any such substitution, but simply by the juxtaposition of tenor and vehicle, as in the Budding Fig Tree (Lk 13:6–9) taken with its prior context, and in the following metaphor in which the tenor is a king and the vehicle includes three animals (Pr 30:29–31):

> There are three things that are stately in their stride,
> > four that move with stately bearing:
> the lion, mighty among beasts,
> > who retreats before nothing;
> a strutting rooster, a he-goat,
> > and a king with his army around him.

Jesus' simplest metaphors generally invite the hearer's intuitive response (e.g., Lk 13:25: "Once the owner of the house gets up and closes the door, you will stand outside knocking and pleading, 'Sir, open the door for us'"); but his argumentative metaphors, usually more elaborate, are PARABLES evoking a reasoned response (e.g., Mk 12:1–12: the Tenants).

Motif. A building block for literature (e.g., a situation, event, or focus of interest) so effective that it frequently recurs with diverse functions in various literary works. Examples of motifs in the parables are the *journey* in the Good Samaritan (Lk 10:25–37), the unexpected *discoveries* in the Weeds, the Hidden Treasure, and the Pearl (Mt 13:24–30, 36–45), the contrast of *good and evil characters* in the Talents (Mt 25:14–30) and the Sheep and Goats (Mt 25:31–46).

Narrative. A speaker or writer's telling or relation of causally linked events; the term is synonymous with *story*. Because narrative has a chronological structure it is distinct from other kinds of DISCOURSE such as the *essay* and the *speech* with their logical organization. Because a narrative relates events by telling in words only, it is also distinct from the mode of discourse known as *drama* which portrays events by showing through bodily representation.

Parable. A saying that is labeled *parable* in one of the Gospels, or any similar saying of Jesus. It expresses or implies the logic of ANALOGY in the language of either SIMILE or METAPHOR elaborated into a form of ALLEGORY that is selectively, but not pervasively, symbolic. Often this allegorical elaboration of the IMAGE of a parable is NARRATIVE—usually creating a STORY-PARABLE, but occasionally an EXAMPLE-STORY. Some parables, however, are not stories but SIMILITUDES, *hypothetical* or merely *descriptive* IMAGES. Jesus' images are drawn realistically from human life or the phenomena of the natural world, though often characterized by some uncommon features, usually symbolic. Because the parables are a genre of *form*, identified by the formal characteristics of analogy, their substance may embody various genres identified by *content*, such as COMEDY, TRAGEDY, RIDDLE, PROVERB, TAUNT, and BYWORD. Unlike the free-standing "parables" of Kafka and others, which encourage the reader's freely improvised interpretations, a parable of Jesus always invites interpretation as the innermost component in a system of concentric literary structures: *Bible* > *New Testament* > *Gospel* > the evangelist's *story* of a particular occasion > Jesus' *discourse* in preaching, teaching, or conversation > *parable.* The parables' invariable moral or spiritual purpose makes them exercises in argumentation intended to evoke from the hearer a reasoned response (e.g., Mk 13:28–29: the Budding Fig Tree)—unlike his simple similes and metaphors, which ask for an intuitive response (e.g., Lk 13:32: Herod as "that fox").

Paradox. A RHETORICAL effect created by language that involves an apparent contradiction while conveying a less obvious and essentially self-coherent truth, e.g., "Unless a grain of wheat falls into the earth and dies, it remains alone; but if it dies, it bears much fruit. He who loves his life loses it, and he who hates his life in this world will keep it for eternal life" (Jn 12:24–25).

Parallelism. A rhetorical device of juxtaposing words, phrases, or sentences that are wholly or partly similar in form or content, e.g., "Some seed fell along the path. . . . Other seed fell on rocky ground" (Mk 4:4–5).

Plot. The pattern of events in a NARRATIVE, artfully arranged to create in the audience successive senses of expectation, complication, CLIMAX, and RESOLUTION.

Point of Resemblance. See TENOR.

Point of View. The psychological perspective from which an audience is permitted by the author to perceive the characters, events, and other features of a story: sometimes limited to what one of the characters can see, know, and relate, sometimes reflecting the perspective of two or more characters, and sometimes "omniscient," i.e., unrestricted by any of the factors that limit a real-life individual's ability to know and tell the whole truth. In relating the wanderings of the Lost Son, for example, Jesus may have deliberately restricted the audience's point of view to the prodigal's perspective, so that they would share his surprise at the opportunity that arises from the father's divergent perspective and unexpected actions (Lk 15:11–32).

Proportional Analogy. See ANALOGY.

Proverb. A wise saying in a brief, apt, and memorable form. When a proverb involves an ANALOGY it is a kind of PARABLE (e.g., 1Sa 10:9–13; and Lk 4:23: "Physician, heal yourself").

Resolution. In any plotted NARRATIVE such as the parables, the conclusion and closure that ordinarily are brought to the conflicts and complications that constitute the bulk of the plot. Because resolution is so common in narrative that we automatically expect it, there is always some special significance to be found in the ending of a story where the resolution is suspended—as in the parable of the Lost Son (Lk 15:11–32) and in Matthew's version of the Tenants (Mt 21:33–46).

Rhetoric. The artful use of language to persuade or otherwise influence an audience. Since virtually any feature of language can be exploited thus, there are many hundreds of identifiable *rhetorical devices* (e.g., ALLEGORY, ALLUSION, ANALOGY, CHIASMUS, ELLIPSIS, END STRESS, HYPERBOLE, IRONY, MEIOSIS, PARALLELISM) and an even larger number of resulting *rhetorical effects.*

Riddle. As a kind of PARABLE, an ANALOGY that is deliberately made enigmatic by the omission (ELLIPSIS) of the TENOR (e.g., Jdg 14:14; and Mk 4:3–8: the Sower) or of the POINT OF RESEMBLANCE.

Sensory Effect. A stimulus to an audience's imagination, created by DICTION denoting something that can be seen, heard, or otherwise perceived by the senses (e.g., Mt 7:27: "The rain came down, the streams rose, and the winds blew").

Setting. The physical environment in which the action of a NARRATIVE occurs—in the parables, usually described only when it contributes significantly to Jesus' meaning, e.g., the road to Jericho in the Good Samaritan (Lk 10:30).

Signal of Comparison. A word or phrase in an ANALOGY that expressly indicates that a comparison is in progress: most commonly *like, as, so,* or *likewise* (e.g., Lk 10:18: "I saw Satan fall like lightning from heaven").

Simile. An ANALOGY of equation in which the presence of a comparison is expressed directly by *like, as, so,* or some similar SIGNAL OF COMPARISON. (Contrast METAPHOR: an analogy in which the act of comparison is only implied.) Jesus' simplest similes generally invited the hearer's intuitive response (e.g., Lk 10:18: "I saw Satan fall like lightning from heaven"); but his similes of argumentation, usually more elaborate, are PARABLES evoking a discursively rational response (e.g., Lk 17:7–10: the Unworthy Servants).

Similitude. A parable that is not elaborated sufficiently to constitute a STORY-PARABLE, but which is either purely *descriptive* (e.g., Mt 23:27–28: Whitewashed Sepulchers) or else *hypothetical* (e.g., Lk 11:11–13: the Asking Son).

Sitz im Leben. A German phrase denoting the "situation in life" of Jesus' parables, other teachings, and actions—that is, the specific cultural, political, social, religious, and personal context in which he uttered a particular saying.

Soliloquy. A speech in NARRATIVE or drama that is delivered aloud but not directed to any hearer; an oral expression of one's private thoughts, e.g., the Rich Fool's "I will tear down my barns and build bigger ones" (Lk 12:18).

Story. See NARRATIVE.

Story-Parable. A PARABLE in which the basic ANALOGY is elaborated (in the manner of ALLEGORY*)* beyond mere pictorial description or hypothetical instance, so as to include a PLOT with one or more characters, comprising a full-fledged NARRATIVE either very brief indeed (e.g., Mt 13:44: the Hidden Treasure) or somewhat longer (e.g., Lk 15:11–32: the Lost Son), but never on the scale of the modern short story.

Symbol. A person or thing, event or place, that is employed by a speaker or writer to signify some meaning besides itself. In Jesus' PARABLES any feature of the VEHICLE is a symbol if it stands for some corresponding feature of the TENOR; and the whole vehicle of a parable may be called a symbol for the whole tenor.

Taunt. A kind of PARABLE that expresses satisfaction about evildoers receiving their just deserts (e.g., Is 14:4–21; and Mt 21:33–46: the Tenants).

Tenor, Vehicle, and Point of Resemblance. The chief components of ANALOGY, a kind of comparison that is particularly suited to illustration or argument because of two special features.

First, in other kinds of comparisons (e.g., "Your house is exactly like my house") the two things compared are equally significant components of the subject, because the speaker's end or purpose encompasses them both alike. By contrast, in the logic of analogy only one of the two things being compared constitutes the speaker's purpose or end (this is the *tenor* of the comparison), while the other thing being compared has a subordinate function as an instrument or means to the speaker's end of "conveying" the significance of the tenor (thus we call this half of the comparison the *vehicle*). For example, the grain of mustard seed that grew into a tree is a vehicle that Jesus used to say something about his tenor, the kingdom of God (Lk 13:18–19: "What is the kingdom of God like? . . . It is like a mustard seed, which a man took and planted in his garden. It grew, became a tree, and the birds of the air perched in its branches"). This feature specially serves the purpose of illustration because a speaker can lead an audience from the known to the unknown—from something more familiar, such as the vehicle of mustard, to something less familiar, such as the tenor of the kingdom.

Second, in other kinds of comparisons (e.g., "Your house is exactly like my house") the two things compared may be alike in every respect. By contrast, in the logic of analogy there may be only one *point of resemblance* between the two things compared; and the two things are never alike in every respect—hence the proverb that every analogy breaks down somewhere. For example, the prodigal's father is like God (Lk 15:11–32) in love and forgiveness, but not in power, wisdom, eternal existence, etc. (*Point of resemblance*, then, denotes some symbolically significant respect in which the *tenor* and *vehicle* of an analogy are alike.) This feature specially serves the purpose of argument because it permits a speaker to focus an audience's attention on one (or a few) key feature(s) of the subject—specifically, the *point(s) of resemblance* between the *tenor* and the *vehicle*.

Scholars sometimes use other terms for *tenor* and *vehicle* respectively: theme and image, reality-part and picture-part, or (in German) *Sache* and *Bild*. The *point of resemblance* has also been known by the Latin phrase *tertium comparationis* because it is the "third [component] of the comparison."

Tertium Comparationis. See POINT OF RESEMBLANCE.

Tone. The effect of language upon an audience's emotions; to be distinguished from *theme*, the effect of language upon an audience's rational processes.

Tragedy. A kind of drama (or in broader use, of NARRATIVE, e.g., Chaucer's "Monk's Tale") that culminates, for the principal characters, in a catastrophe of loss and expulsion—almost always death. In its classic form tragedy portrays a hero or heroine whose tragic flaw of moral character prompts some fatal choice(s) bringing about the catastrophe. This tragic plot pattern, of a hopeful enterprise inadvertently brought to disaster (contrast COMEDY), is found in some parables, e.g., the Unmerciful Servant (Mt 18:23–35), the Tenants (Mk 12:1–12), and the Rich Fool (Lk 12:13–21). Because Jesus' message concerns the significance of accepting or rejecting God's commands, more parables are *tragicomic*—that is, the ending is happy for some and unhappy for others, e.g., the Two Builders (Mt 7:24–27), the Two Sons (Mt 21:28–32), the Two Ways (Mt 7:13–14), the Two Debtors (Lk 7:41–47), the Ten Maidens (Mt 25:1–13), the Talents (Mt 25:14–30), the Sheep and Goats (Mt 25:31–46), the Great Supper (Lk 14:15–24).

Triplet. See DOUBLET.

Vehicle. See TENOR.

BIBLIOGRAPHY

Achtemeier, P. Mark. "Matthew 13:1–23." *Interpretation* 44 (1990): 61–65.

Arndt, William F. *The Gospel According to St. Luke*. St. Louis: Concordia, 1956.

Bailey, Kenneth Ewing. *Poet and Peasant: A Literary Cultural Approach to the Parables in Luke*. Grand Rapids: Eerdmans, 1976.

———. *Through Peasant Eyes: More Lucan Parables, Their Culture and Style*. Grand Rapids: Eerdmans, 1980.

Baird, J. Arthur. "A Pragmatic Approach to Parable Exegesis: Some New Evidence on Mark 4:11, 33–34." *Journal of Biblical Literature* 76 (1957): 201–7.

Bauckham, Richard. "The Rich Man and Lazarus: The Parable and the Parallels." *New Testament Studies* 37 (1991): 225–46.

Beare, Francis Wright. *The Gospel According to Matthew*. San Francisco: Harper & Row, 1981.

Beavis, Mary Ann. "Ancient Slavery as an Interpretive Context for the New Testament Servant Parables with Special Reference to the Unjust Steward (Luke 16.1–8)." *Journal of Biblical Literature* 111 (1992): 37–54.

———. "Parable and Fable." *Catholic Biblical Quarterly* 52 (1990): 473–98.

Black, Matthew. "The Parables as Allegory." *Bulletin of the John Rylands Library,* 42 (1960): 273–87.

Blomberg, Craig L. *Interpreting the Parables*. Downers Grove, Ill.: Inter-Varsity Press, 1990.

Boswell, James. *Life of Johnson*. Oxford: Oxford University Press, 1953.

Boucher, Madeleine. *The Mysterious Parable: A Literary Study*. Washington, D.C.: The Catholic Biblical Association of America, 1977.

Bowie, Walter Russell et al. Exposition of Luke 15:8–10, 9–10. *Interpreter's Bible* 8:268–69. New York and Nashville: Abingdon, 1952.

Breech, James. *The Silence of Jesus: The Authentic Voice of the Historical Man*. Philadelphia: Fortress, 1983.

Brown, Raymond E. "Parable and Allegory Reconsidered." *Novum Testamentum* 5 (1962): 36–45.

Browne, Laurence E. *The Parables of the Gospels in the Light of Modern Criticism*. Cambridge: Cambridge University Press, 1913.

Buttrick, George A. Exposition of Matthew 13:3–8. *Interpreter's Bible* 7:408–9. New York and Nashville: Abingdon, 1951.

Cadoux, A. T. *The Parables of Jesus: Their Art and Use*. London: James Clarke, 1931.

Carlston, Charles E. *The Parables of the Triple Tradition*. Philadelphia: Fortress, 1975.

Crossan, John Dominic. *Finding Is the First Act: Trove Folktales and Jesus' Treasure Parable*. Philadelphia: Fortress; Missoula: Scholars, 1979.

_____. *In Parables: The Challenge of the Historical Jesus*. New York: Harper & Row, 1973.

Culley, Robert C. "Response to Daniel Patte." In *Semiology and Parables*. Edited by Daniel Patte, pp. 151–58. Pittsburgh: Pickwick, 1976.

Derrett, J. Duncan M. *Law in the New Testament*. London: Darton, Longman & Todd, 1970.

Dodd, Charles H. *Historical Tradition in the Fourth Gospel*. Cambridge: Cambridge University Press, 1963.

_____. *The Parables of the Kingdom*. London: Nisbet & Co., 1935.

Donahue, John R. *The Gospel in Parable: Metaphor, Narrative, and Theology in the Synoptic Gospels*. Philadelphia: Fortress, 1988.

Donfried, Karl Paul. "The Allegory of the Ten Virgins (Matt 25:1–13) as a Summary of Matthean Theology." *Journal of Biblical Literature* 93 (1974): 415–28.

Downing, F. Gerald. "The Ambiguity of 'The Pharisee and the Toll-Collector' (Luke 18:9–14) in the Greco-Roman World of Late Antiquity." *Catholic Biblical Quarterly* 54 (1992): 80–99.

Drury, John. *The Parables in the Gospels: History and Allegory*. New York: Crossroads, 1985.

Fay, Greg. "Introduction to Incomprehension: The Literary Structure of Mark 4:1–34." *Catholic Biblical Quarterly* 51 (1989): 65–81.

Frye, Northrop. *Anatomy of Criticism*. Princeton: Princeton University Press, 1957.

Fuchs, Ernst. *Studies of the Historical Jesus*, trans. Andrew Scobie. London: SCM Press, 1964.

Funk, Robert W. *Jesus as Precursor*. Philadelphia: Fortress; Missoula: Scholars, 1975.

————. *Language, Hermeneutic, and Word of God*. New York: Harper & Row, 1966.

————. *Parables and Presence*. Philadelphia: Fortress, 1982.

Gerhardsson, Birger. "If We Do Not Cut the Parables Out of Their Frames." *New Testament Studies* 37 (1991): 321–35.

Gilbert, W. S., and Arthur Sullivan. *The Complete Plays*. New York: Modern Library, 1936.

Goulder, M. D. *Midrash and Lection in Matthew*. London: SPCK, 1974.

Gundry, Robert H. *Matthew: A Commentary on His Literary and Theological Art*. Grand Rapids: Eerdmans, 1982.

Heard, Warren. "Luke's Attitude Toward the Rich and the Poor." *Trinity Journal*, n.s. (1988): 47–80.

Heil, John Paul. "Reader-Response and the Narrative Context of the Parables About Growing Seed in Mark 4:1–34." *Catholic Biblical Quarterly* 54 (1992): 271–86.

Henry, Matthew. *Commentary on the Holy Bible*. 6 vols. Old Tappan, N.J.: Revell, c. 1970.

Holmgren, Fredrick C. "The Pharisee and the Tax Collector: Luke 18:9–14 and Deuteronomy 26:1–15." *Interpretation* 48 (1994): 252–60.

Huffman, Norman A. "Atypical Features in the Parables of Jesus." *Journal of Biblical Literature* 97 (1978): 207–20.

Hunter, Archibald M. *Interpreting the Parables*. Philadelphia: Westminster Press, 1960.

Ireland, Dennis J. "A History of Recent Interpretation of the Parable of the Unjust Steward (Luke 16:1–13)." *Westminster Theological Journal* 51 (1989): 293–318.

Jeremias, Joachim. *The Parables of Jesus,* 2d rev. ed. Translated by S. H. Hooke. New York: Charles Scribner's Sons, 1972.

Jones, Geraint Vaughan. *The Art and Truth of the Parables: A Study in Their Literary Form and Modern Interpretation.* London: SPCK, 1964.

Jülicher, Adolf. *Die Gleichnisreden Jesu,* Tübingen. Vol. 1: 1888, 2d ed. 1899. Vol. 2: 1889. 2 vols. Reprinted Tübingen: J. C. B. Mohr, 1910. Except as otherwise indicated, all citations of Jülicher refer to this work.

_____. "Parable." *Encyclopedia Biblica* (1902), 3:3563–67.

Kahlfeld, Heinrich. *Parables and Instructions in the Gospels.* Translated by Arlene Swidler. New York: Herder and Herder, 1966.

Kilgallen, John H. "Provocation in Luke 4, 23–24." *Biblica* 70 (1989): 511–16.

_____. "The Return of the Unclean Spirit (Luke 11, 24–26)." *Biblica* 74 (1993): 45–59.

Kingsbury, Jack Dean. *The Parables of Jesus in Matthew 13: A Study in Redaction-Criticism.* Richmond: John Knox, 1969.

Kissinger, Warren S. *The Parables of Jesus: A History of Interpretation and Bibliography.* Metuchen, N.J., and London: Scarecrow Press, 1979.

Kistemaker, Simon J. *The Parables of Jesus.* Grand Rapids: Baker, 1980.

Kloppenborg, John S. "The Dishonoured Master (Luke 16, 1–8a)." *Biblica* 70 (1989): 474–95.

Kümmel, Werner Georg. *The New Testament: The History of the Investigation of Its Problems.* Translated by S. McLean Gilmour and Howard C. Kee. Nashville: Abingdon, 1972.

Lambrecht, Jan. *Once More Astonished: The Parables of Jesus.* New York: Crossroad, 1981.

Levin, Harry. "General Introduction." *The Riverside Shakespeare.* Boston: Houghton Mifflin, 1974.

Lewis, C. S. *Rehabilitations and Other Essays,* 1939. Reprint Folcroft, Pa.: Folcroft, 1973.

_____. *Christian Reflections,* ed. Walter Hooper. Grand Rapids: Eerdmans, 1967.

Lincoln, Abraham. "Speech Delivered at Springfield. . . ." *The Life and Writings of Abraham Lincoln.* Edited by Philip Van Doren Stern, 428–39. New York: Random House, n.d.

Linnemann, Eta. *Parables of Jesus: Introduction and Exposition.* Translated by John Sturdy. London: SPCK, 1966.

Longman, Tremper, III. *Literary Approaches to Biblical Interpretation.* Grand Rapids: Zondervan, 1987.

Moessner, David P. *Lord of the Banquet: The Literary and Theological Significance of the Lukan Travel Narrative.* Minneapolis: Fortress, 1989.

Montefiore, C. G. *The Synoptic Gospels,* 2d ed. 2 vols. N.p., 1927. Reprint. New York: KTAV, 1968.

Moorman, John R. H. *The Path to Glory: Studies in the Gospel According to Saint Luke.* London: SPCK and Seabury, 1960.

More, Saint Thomas. *Utopia.* Translated and edited by Robert M. Adams. New York: Norton, 1975.

Mowry, L. "Parable." *Interpreter's Dictionary of the Bible,* 3:649–54.

Noorda, S. J. "«Cure Yourself, Doctor!» (Luke 4,23) Classical Parallels to an Alleged Saying of Jesus." *Logia: Les Paroles de Jesus—The Sayings of Jesus.* Edited by Joël Delobel. Louvain University Press, 1982.

Oesterly, W. O. E. *The Gospel Parables in the Light of Their Jewish Background.* London: SPCK; New York: Macmillan, 1936.

Parrott, Douglas M. "The Dishonest Steward (Luke 16:1–8a) and Luke's Special Parable Collection." *New Testament Studies* 37 (1991): 499–515.

Patte, Daniel. *What Is Structural Exegesis?* Philadelphia: Fortress, 1976.

Perrin, Norman. *Jesus and the Language of the Kingdom.* Philadelphia: Fortress, 1976.

_____. *Rediscovering the Teaching of Jesus.* New York: Harper & Row, 1967.

Resseguie, James L. "Luke 7:36–50: Making the Familiar Seem Strange." *Interpretation* 46 (1992): 285–90.

Ridderbos, H. N. *The Bible Student's Commentary—Matthew.* Translated by Ray Togtman. Grand Rapids: Zondervan, 1987.

Scharlemann, Martin H. *Proclaiming the Parables*. St. Louis: Concordia, 1963.

Scott, Bernard Brandon. *Hear Then the Parable: A Commentary on the Parables of Jesus*. Minneapolis: Fortress, 1989.

Sellew, Philip. "Interior Monologue as a Narrative Device in the Parables of Luke." *Journal of Biblical Literature* 111 (1992): 239–53.

Shakespeare, William. *The Riverside Shakespeare*. Boston: Houghton Mifflin, 1974.

Sider, John W. "The Meaning of *Parabole* in the Usage of the Synoptic Evangelists." *Biblica* 62 (1981): 453–70.

_____. "Nurturing Our Nurse: Literary Scholars and Biblical Exegesis." *Christianity and Literature* 32 (1982): 15–21.

_____. "Rediscovering the Parables: The Logic of the Jeremias Tradition." *Journal of Biblical Literature* 102 (1983): 61–83.

_____. "Interpreting the Hid Treasure." *Christian Scholar's Review* 13 (1984): 360–72.

_____. "Proportional Analogy in the Gospel Parables." *New Testament Studies* 31 (1985): 1–23.

_____. "The Parables." In *A Complete Literary Guide to the Bible*. Edited by Leland Ryken and Tremper Longman III. Grand Rapids: Zondervan, 1993.

Siker, Jeffrey S. "'First to the Gentiles': A Literary Analysis of Luke 4:16–30." *Journal of Biblical Literature* 111 (1992): 76–81.

Silva, Moisés. *Has the Church Misread the Bible? The History of Interpretation in the Light of Current Issues*. Grand Rapids: Zondervan, 1987.

Smith, B. T. D. *The Parables of the Synoptic Gospels: A Critical Study*. Cambridge: Cambridge University Press, 1937.

Stein, Robert H. *An Introduction to the Parables of Jesus*. Philadelphia: Westminster, 1981.

Talbert, Charles H. *Reading Luke: A Literary and Theological Commentary on the Third Gospel*. New York: Crossroad, 1984.

TeSelle, Sallie McFague. *Speaking in Parables: A Study in Metaphor and Theology*. Philadelphia: Fortress, 1975.

Tolbert, Mary Ann. "How the Gospel of Mark Builds Character." *Interpretation* 47 (1993): 347–75.

_____. *Perspectives on the Parables*. Philadelphia: Fortress, 1979.

Via, Dan Otto, Jr. *The Parables: Their Literary and Existential Dimension*. Philadelphia: Fortress, 1967.

Wilson, R. McL. "Mark." *Peake's Commentary on the Bible*. Edited by Matthew Black. London: Thomas Nelson, 1962.

Young, Brad H. *Jesus and His Jewish Parables: Rediscovering the Roots of Jesus' Teaching*. New York: Paulist, 1989.

INDEX TO
BIBLICAL REFERENCES

INDEX TO
PARABLES AND OTHER COMPARISONS OF JESUS

INDEX TO
AUTHORS